Baby & Child
Vegetarian Recipes

Baby & Child Vegetarian Recipes

Over 150 healthy and delicious dishes
for your young family

CAROL TIMPERLEY

Illustrations by
STEPHEN MAY

EBURY PRESS
LONDON

7 9 10 8 6

Text copyright © Carol Timperley 1997, 2009
Illustrations copyright © Stephen May 1997
This edition copyright © Eddison Sadd Editions 2009

First published in the United Kingdom in 1997 by Ebury Press.
This revised edition published in 2009 by
Ebury Press
Random House
20 Vauxhall Bridge Road
London SW1V 2SA

Random House South Africa (Pty) Ltd
Endulini, 5A Jubilee Road
Parktown 2193, South Africa

Random House UK Limited Reg. No. 954009

A CIP catalogue record for this book is available from the British Library

ISBN 978-0-09-185300-6

AN EDDISON•SADD EDITION
Edited, designed and produced by
Eddison Sadd Editions Limited
St Chad's House, 148 King's Cross Road
London WC1X 9DH

Phototypeset in Novarese BT using QuarkXPress on Apple Macintosh.
Printed and bound in Thailand

CONTENTS

INTRODUCTION

When my son was first born, I was visited in hospital by a resolutely childless and cynical chum. She cast a dismissive glance at the bundle that I, like all new mothers, firmly believed to be the most perfect human being ever created, helped herself to a glass of champagne and commented, 'You do realise that it's all guilt and worry from here onwards?'. Naturally, in my euphoria, I dismissed her comment as sour grapes. Four years later the resonance of those words is all too apparent. The desire to do the very best for our children, combined with a barrage of well-meaning advice, can conspire to make even the most competent parents feel inadequate at times. This is particularly true of diet. My aim in writing this book, however, is to give parents a practical and reassuring guide to vegetarian food, to help dispel the uncertainties that often surround vegetarian eating, and give parents confidence that they are providing the best possible diet for their children.

While it has long been recognised that we are what we eat, expert opinion now suggests that the degenerative diseases which plague our middle years are the direct result of a poor diet in childhood. Indeed, research in America has revealed children as young as eleven years old with furred arteries and raised cholesterol levels; small time bombs waiting to explode into disaster zones of ill-health. In the light of this knowledge, it makes sense to give your child the best possible nutritional start in life.

It is my firm belief that the best possible nutritional start for a child means a vegetarian diet. As a parent, whether your reason for following a meat-free diet is ethical, environmental or a matter of pure preference, from the point of view of your child's health the statistics speak for themselves. Research has proven that vegetarians suffer 50 per cent less heart disease and 40 per cent fewer cancers than meat eaters, and are 20 per cent less prone to premature mortality. Vegetarians also enjoy lower incidences of all manner of diet-related disorders, from hypertension to haemorrhoids, food-poisoning to unsightly, health-threatening excess body fat.

Yet, while adults are increasingly turning towards a vegetarian diet, with the approval of health professionals, there is relatively little practical advice or support available for parents who wish to bring up their children as vegetarians. In fact, one of the medical textbooks I consulted in researching this book lists vegetarianism along with Zen Macrobiotic Diets under 'Dietary Abnormalities'! Such prejudice is not uncommon among the medical profession. My son's father is a cardiac surgeon and I have known more than one of his highly qualified colleagues to be more phased at the prospect of a vegetarian dinner guest than a multiple coronary artery bypass. The situation is not helped by the 'evangelical vegetarians' whose purist doctrine necessitates special shopping trips and hours of pounding pulses. I hope that the advice offered in this book falls somewhere between the two extremes. (It is aimed at vegetarians, who consume milk and milk products, with or without eggs. Vegan mothers should seek further advice, perhaps from The Vegetarian Society.)

There is a common myth (perpetrated by those who perceive a vegetarian diet as a life-time sentence to a steak-shaped gap on the dinner plate) that meat-free meals are time consuming and complicated to make, and nutritiously inadequate. As all vegetarians know, this idea could not be more misguided. What could be quicker and simpler than a nutri-tious meal of beans on toast, or even a cheese sandwich? Furthermore, vegetarian babies tend to be bigger, brighter and more resilient than their meat-eating peers.

As a busy working mother I understand all too well the pressures and constraints associ-ated with juggling a career and family life. This is why you won't find in the following chapters any recipes which require soaking lentils or other lengthy preparation processes. Nor am I opposed to the occasional jar of puréed veg-etables or cube of chocolate – it's the general landscape, not the immediate outlook, that counts when feeding children. This said, when pressed for time, I would far rather my son ate a banana, a yoghurt, and toast and Marmite than any of the so-called kids' specials on offer at a supermarket or take-away near me.

If you opt to bring up your child as a vege-tarian for ethical rather than health reasons, you may encounter the attitude that you are selfishly inflicting your own ideals on your child (as though food is the only area in which we make choices on our children's behalf!). In fact, most children instinctively veer towards a veg-etarian diet. After all, meat is a fibrous, lumpy substance which requires effort to chew. Children have to work quite hard to acquire a taste for meat. I well recall one occasion when my son was invited for tea at a small friend's house and was served a pasta sauce containing chicken (I had failed to specify that he did not eat meat). When I called to collect him I was told that he had diligently removed every chunk of chicken from the sauce.

The menu charts included in each chapter are no more than suggestions as to how you might combine recipes and basic foods to pro-vide your child with a balanced diet. Provided you offer a wide variety of fresh foods, both cooked and raw, and observe the general prin-ciples of keeping sugar and salt to a minimum, you cannot go far wrong. Above all, bear in mind that, while food is primarily sustenance, a healthy diet of carefully, if simply, prepared fresh foods is a unique expression of our connection with our families, friends and environment. An appreciation of good food is one of the greatest of all gifts you can give your child.

• •

CHAPTER ONE

From Milk to Solids

Babies, it seems to me, are living proof of the theories of both chaos and perpetual motion. This is as true of your baby's eating patterns as it is of every other aspect of their development. No sooner have you got to grips with the whole milk business (when, how much, the best method of winding), than they decide it's time to move on to the next stage. Just as you are certain that mashed banana never fails to please, they obstinately refuse anything and everything containing the faintest trace of it. It's almost as though they have an infallible instinct for detecting the split second that you feel really confident and they decide at that point to upset the apple-purée cart before you become complacent. And the more uptight mum gets, the better junior enjoys the game. When it comes to feeding children, if there is one golden rule it must be to remain relaxed about the whole process.

For at least the first six months of your baby's life, the major source of nourishment is milk, which contains all the protein, vitamins, minerals and fat required for healthy growth. Experts agree that breast milk is best for a variety of reasons – not least because it adapts to your growing baby's needs while also containing valuable antibodies and antibacterial agents to help increase resistance to disease. And, should you need convincing of the important role diet plays in development right from the start, recent studies to emerge from America suggest that children who were breast-fed as babies, even for just a few weeks, perform better academically at school than their bottle-fed peers.

From mum's point of view, breast feeding has the added advantages of costing nothing, and instantly providing milk at the correct temperature. If you breast feed your baby, it is important to pay close attention to your own diet and ensure that you eat plenty of vitamin- and calcium-rich foods (see the lists of such foods on the following pages) and also drink plenty of water.

Even if you do breast feed, at some point during the first year of your baby's life you will probably want to substitute bottles for at least some of the milk feeds. (Not all breast-fed babies will accept a bottle. Some just refuse and get distraught and hungry, no matter who gives the bottle, or how early. Others readily accept a bottle, and some even prefer a bottle to the breast.) If you do decide to substitute a bottle, you should always choose a proprietary formula milk as this is better suited to your baby's nutritional requirements than cow's milk. Always read the label carefully (some formulas contain animal fats which are unacceptable to strict vegetarians – your health visitor should be able to advise) and follow the instructions for making up the formula to the letter, as the wrong concentration of powder to fluid can be harmful. Use freshly boiled tap water, never bottled water which may contain harmful mineral and salt deposits.

Once your child is twelve months old you may safely introduce full-fat cow's milk as a drink. Cow's milk is suitable for cooking purposes from about six months, as are other dairy products such as cheese, yoghurt and fromage frais. (However, there are benefits in continuing to use formula or breast milk even in cooking after six months as it does provide additional nutrients not found in cow's milk.)

For as long as you continue to use bottles (many young children, my own son included, seem to find a bedtime bottle comforting for up to three years) you must continue to sterilise them because of the risk of bacteria. Although not strictly necessary if your child has a good appetite, it is wise to ensure that at least 600 ml/1 pint of milk a day is taken for the first two years. For vegetarian children especially, it is a valuable source of protein and vitamin B12.

A Matter of Substance

For a host of reasons (see Chapter Two), it is not a good idea to attempt to wean your baby too early, and certainly never before the age of four months. However, by about six months you should be introducing solids because it is thought that the supplies of iron with which your baby is born begin to run out at about this time. Of course, the foods you offer your baby at this initial stage of weaning will be anything but solid, but they represent a marked contrast to milk, in texture and taste. Simple non-wheat cereal (baby rice), fruit and vegetable purées are the ideal supplements to milk. There is no need to concern yourself too much in these early stages with nutritional or calorific values – the idea is really to get your baby used to the business of eating. However, as you progress to the next stage of weaning when solids form a more significant part of your baby's diet, it becomes important to think about food values.

Balancing Act

The phrase 'a balanced diet' seems designed to strike trepidation into the heart of anyone lacking a dietetic qualification or a degree in food science, implying as it does the need for scales, calculators and mathematical equations. In fact, there is no great mystique about a balanced diet. This simply means eating a variety of foods chosen from each of the six major food groups: proteins, carbohydrates, fats, vitamins, minerals and water.

As long as you include at least some of these in your baby's diet each day, the remarkably clever computer that is the body will do the rest. The six major nutrient groups that you need concern yourself with are as follows.

PROTEINS

Protein is essential for the growth and repair of body tissue. Many misconceptions surround the ability of a vegetarian diet to supply adequate amounts of protein for a growing child. The confusion arises because proteins are made up of some 20 amino acids, roughly half of which the body can make itself and the remainder of which (known as essential amino acids) need to be supplied by food. While animal proteins contain all of the essential amino acids, individual plant proteins may contain lower amounts of some of them and therefore need to be eaten in combination.

For vegetarians who eat dairy products this is not a problem and even those who do not eat dairy foods receive more than adequate supplies of amino acids simply by eating a variety of protein foods. In fact, be reassured that it is almost impossible not to eat sufficient protein (assuming sufficient food is eaten), and that most western diets contain more protein than is needed, which could place a strain on the kidneys. Good vegetarian sources of protein include milk and milk products, such as cheese and yoghurt; eggs; soya products, such as tofu and textured vegetable protein; all nuts (see page 14) and seeds; beans and pulses, for example, lentils and kidney beans; and grains, such as wheat, barley and rice.

There was a time when people thought it necessary to balance vegetable proteins so that the exact amount of each amino acid would be present at each meal. This view of 'food combining' is nutritionally out of date, as it is now known that the body has a short-term store of essential amino acids and so a balance of amino acids can be taken over the course of a day rather than at each meal. Vegetarians and vegans eating a mixture of grains, pulses, seeds, nuts and vegetables will be consuming a balance of amino acids without any planning. For vegetarian babies and children, breast milk, formula or cow's milk, eggs, and milk products such as cheese, yoghurt and milk puddings (not cream or butter) provide complete protein. Meals such as beans on toast, nut butter or cheese sandwiches, cereal with milk, and rice with peas, beans or lentils are good examples of simple meals which contain a reasonable balance of amino acids.

CARBOHYDRATES

Carbohydrates are vital for growth and providing energy, and the starchy variety should be the most abundant nutrient in the diets of adults and young children.

However, while large amounts of unrefined carbohydrates (for example, brown bread and pasta, cereals, potato skins, beans and pulses) are desirable for adults, they should be given to children with caution. While avoiding refined sugars (found in sweets, biscuits, cakes and squashes) wherever possible, do bear in mind that high-fibre diets can conflict with the intense nutritional requirements of growing infants, filling them up before they have obtained sufficient nutrients for healthy growth and development. Provided your child eats plenty of fruit, there is absolutely nothing wrong in allowing meals to include white bread and pasta rather than the wholemeal versions (there may even be certain advantages). Good sources of carbohydrate include all fruits and vegetables, breakfast cereals, bread and pasta; starchy vegetables such as potatoes and peas; and lentils and pulses.

As children get older, some wholemeal foods, such as brown bread, pasta, rice and wholemeal cereals, should be eaten to avoid constipation, promote healthy eating habits and also provide a useful source of B vitamins. It is best to avoid any products with added bran, such as bran-flake cereals, which can cause digestive problems and prevent the absorption of some minerals.

FATS

Despite having become almost as taboo as the other F-word in recent times, fats provide a concentrated source of energy and, in young children, they are important for the healthy development of the brain and nervous system. In fact, it is saturated fats, implicated in many of the degenerative diseases to which the Western world is prone, which give this necessary food group its bad reputation.

For vegetarians, the good news is that saturated fat comes almost exclusively from animal products, so, providing that you regulate the amount of dairy produce in your child's diet and use good-quality vegetable oils such as olive oil wherever possible for cooking, you will be making a great contribution to safeguarding his or her future health. However, it is vital that you do not attempt to feed your child low-fat dairy products for at least the first two years because milk fat is a valuable source of both energy and fat-soluble vitamins. In addition to dairy products, other good sources of fat are vegetable oils such as soya, sunflower and corn; olive oil; margarine (non-hydrogenated varieties are best), avocados and nuts.

Hydrogenated fats should be avoided for babies, children, pregnant and breast-feeding women, because they contain trans fatty acids which can interfere with the essential fatty acids vital for healthy brain development. This is particularly important for vegetarians as their bodies make these nutrients rather than obtaining them from fish oil. Hydrogenated fats are found in some margarines and commercial food products, so read the labels.

VITAMINS

Vitamins are essential for correct body functioning, and certain antioxidant vitamins (A, C and E) are now thought to play a major role in protecting against cancer. There are two main types of vitamins: fat soluble and water soluble. The fat-soluble vitamins (A, D, E and K) can be stored by the body, but the water-soluble vitamins (C and B complex, except B12) cannot and therefore need to be supplied on a daily basis. Because they dissolve in water, this group of vitamins can be destroyed by overzealous cooking. Fruit and vegetables should be lightly cooked, preferably steamed, or served raw if possible. Vitamin K is made by bacteria in the gut, but, as new-born babies do not have these bacteria, they are routinely offered

VITAMINS IN FOCUS

VITAMIN A
Necessary for growth, healthy skin and tooth enamel, and good vision. Good sources:
Carrots • Spinach • Green Leafy Vegetables • Watercress • Peppers • Dried Apricots

VITAMIN B GROUP
Necessary for growth, for the conversion of food into energy, a healthy nervous system and for the formation of red blood cells. Good sources:
Green Leafy Vegetables • Wheatgerm • Whole Grains • Beansprouts • Bananas • Avocados • Mushrooms • Peanuts • Yeast Extract, e.g. Vegemite • TVP • Fortified Breakfast Cereals • Margarine • Dairy Products

VITAMIN C
Necessary for growth, healthy body tissue, wound healing and resistance to infection. Also aids iron absorption so is especially important for vegetarians, as plant-derived iron deposits are less readily absorbed than those found in meat. Good sources:
Green Leafy Vegetables • Broccoli • Cabbage • Peppers • Parsley • Potatoes • Peas • Citrus and Berry Fruits

VITAMIN D
Necessary for the formation of healthy bones and teeth. Can be manufactured by the body when the skin is exposed to sunlight, but it is also found in:
Dairy Products • Fortified Cereals • Margarine

VITAMIN E
Necessary for the maintenance of the body's cell structure. Good sources:
Vegetable Oils • Wheatgerm • Nuts • Seeds • Avocados

VITAMIN K
Necessary for blood-clotting. Good sources:
Green Leafy Vegetables • Vegetable Oils • Whole Grains

vitamin K orally or by injection at birth.

Because fruit and vegetables are rich in vitamins, vegetarian children tend to have an adequate vitamin intake without the need to resort to the supplements routinely offered to children by many clinics. Vitamin B12 and vitamin D, which are frequently cited as areas of concern for vegetarians, are present in adequate amounts in all dairy products, in fortified breakfast cereals and, in the case of vitamin D, in most vegetable margarines.

MINERALS IN FOCUS

IRON

Iron is necessary for the formation of red blood cells. While it is present in many plant foods, the body does not absorb iron from plant sources as readily as from animal sources. A diet rich in wholefoods compounds this problem. However, if vitamin C is taken at the same time as iron-rich foods, absorption is markedly increased. Good sources of iron:

Tofu • Beans • Pulses • Spinach • Cabbage • Wheatgerm • Whole Grains • Dried Fruits

CALCIUM

Calcium is necessary for the formation of healthy bones and teeth and is therefore particularly important for growing children. Good sources of calcium:

Dairy Products • Tofu • Green Leafy Vegetables • Almonds • Brazil Nuts • Sesame Seeds

ZINC

Zinc is vital to many body functions, including growth. Good sources of zinc:

Whole Grains • Beans and Pulses • Pumpkin and Sesame Seeds • Dairy Products • Nuts

---

MINERALS

Like vitamins, minerals cannot be manufactured by the body and therefore need to be supplied by the diet. Although the body requires some fifteen different minerals, the three most important in relation to a vegetarian diet are iron, calcium and zinc. Milk and dairy products are very poor sources of iron. Too much cow's milk has been linked to iron-deficiency anaemia in toddlers. Lack of iron is a fairly common problem in the diets of very small children. For vegetarian children under the age of two who like a lot of milk and dairy products, an iron-fortified follow-on milk (from chemists) is recommended (or an iron supplement).

WATER

Up until the age of about six months your baby normally obtains enough fluid from milk. In certain circumstances – for example, in exceptionally hot weather or during a stomach upset – you may wish to offer additional fluid in the form of cooled boiled tap water. If, however, your baby is vomiting and has diarrhoea and these symptoms persist for more than twenty-four hours, you should seek medical advice, as young babies can dehydrate very rapidly, with potentially serious consequences. Once your baby is taking solids, you should offer regular drinks in addition to the milk feeds as long as he or she continues to eat well (some babies have a tendency to fill themselves up with fluids and then refuse their food).

Although there are many commercially available herbal and fruit drinks specifically for babies, all of these are rich in sugar which can harm developing teeth, so water remains the best choice. Should you decide to give fruit juices (if, for example, your baby seems reluctant to take water) always dilute them as much as possible and give them in a trainer cup or beaker (never a bottle) to minimise the risk of damage to teeth. Fizzy drinks of any description are unsuitable for young children.

Allergies and Additives

An allergy is an abnormal reaction to any food or substance. Most typically an allergy manifests itself in the form of rashes, stomach upsets, bodily swelling and hyperactive behaviour. Thankfully, allergies are fairly rare, although some experts do believe that they are on the increase. Common food allergies include dairy products, wheat, citrus fruits and nuts (see below). Where there is a family history of parental allergy, these foods should be introduced with caution.

There is considerable evidence to suggest that babies who are breast-fed are less susceptible to developing allergies, as are those who are weaned slightly later than average. These points may be worth considering if you suspect a hereditary allergy. Many widely used food additives, such as the colouring tartrazine, are associated with allergic reactions in children, so it makes sense to avoid these. More difficult to cope with are allergies to basic foods such as cow's milk, a particular problem for babies who are bottle-fed. Soya milk formulas are available, but are only recommended for babies in exceptional circumstances. If you suspect your baby has an allergy of this kind, consult your paediatrician before changing milk formula.

Food intolerances are conditions where the body is incapable of digesting certain substances. Lactose and gluten intolerance are the most serious, but fortunately they are rare.

HONEY
Do not give honey to children under twelve months, due to the risk of infant botulism. With toddlers and children over one year old, it can be used sparingly.

NUTS
Nuts should always be ground for under-fives because of the risk of choking. There is also concern about nut allergies, which are increasingly common in children and can be severe. Very recent research, as yet not fully accepted, would suggest that there is room for concern, particularly in families with a history of allergies, eczema or asthma. Some researchers suggest that children within such families should refrain from eating nuts until the age of three and that other families would do no harm in introducing them a little later than presently suggested by accepted guidelines.

Soya Milk and Soya Products

Soya milk formulas are only recommended for babies in exceptional circumstances because soya naturally contains high levels of phyto-estrogens which can mimic natural hormones. This may have some benefits for adult women (in protecting against breast cancer), but could upset a baby's delicate hormone balance. At the time of writing, baby-milk manufacturers are looking to reduce the amounts of phyto-estrogens in soya milk formula. Vegan mothers, who avoid all dairy products, have a strong incentive to continue breast feeding for the first two years of life.

It is fine to introduce foods such as tofu (soya bean curd), soya milk, soya burgers and sausages to a child over one as part of a varied vegetarian diet.

A Matter of Convenience

In an ideal world, every morsel that passed our child's lips would be lovingly and freshly prepared from the finest natural ingredients. However, few of us are fortunate enough to manage this. Inevitably, there will be occasions when it is necessary to resort to convenience foods. Try not to torture yourself with guilt when this happens; the occasional packet or jar is not going to adversely affect your baby's growth and development (although relying on such foods exclusively may, if only in relation to his palate).

When buying convenience foods, read the label or packet carefully and reject any foods with a high content of hydrogenated fat, sugar (maltodextrin, dextrose, sucrose), salt or bulking agents such as modified starch. It is now possible to buy organic baby foods in jars and these are preferable to other types. For emergencies, many ordinary food products are suitable for babies: for example, canned baked beans (choose one of the low-sugar, low-salt varieties); canned fruits in natural juice; and canned vegetables such as sweetcorn, peas, and beans in water, without added salt or sugar.

GETTING THE TIMING RIGHT

There are few hard and fast rules about the age at which it magically becomes safe to introduce certain foods. The important thing is to introduce new foods in the order suggested below. The list is intended as a guideline only. By the age of 12 months or so, your baby should be able to enjoy most foods, prepared appropriately (with the exception of whole nuts).

FIRST STAGE OF WEANING: 4–6 MONTHS
Apples • Apricots • Avocados • Bananas • Carrots • Cauliflower • Leeks • Mangoes • Melon • Parsnips • Pears • Potatoes • Rice

SECOND STAGE OF WEANING: 6–9 MONTHS
Aubergines • Beetroot • Berry Fruits • Bread • Broccoli • Cabbage • Celery • Citrus Fruits • Cherries • Courgettes • Dairy Products (butter, cheese, cream, yoghurt, fromage frais) • Grapes • Lentils, refined and puréed • Mushrooms • Oats • Onions • Pasta • Peas • Peppers • Pineapple • Seeds • Sprouts • Tomatoes

THIRD STAGE OF WEANING: 9–12 MONTHS
Beans and Pulses • Nuts, ground (optional) • Peanut Butter • Salads

12 MONTHS AND ABOVE
Full-fat Cow's Milk • Yeast Extract • Seasoning • Honey

Some of the commercially produced cereals are also acceptable for babies and young children; Weetabix, Shredded Wheat and Ready Brek in particular.

Frozen fruit and vegetables make acceptable alternatives to fresh vegetables, and they may be richer in nutrients. If you do use frozen vegetables, choose packets from the bottom of the freezer cabinet (their temperature will be lower than those nearer the top), and pack them in an insulated bag to prevent defrosting on the journey home.

Hygiene

When preparing and cooking food for babies and young children, it is important to be scrupulous about your own and your kitchen hygiene. Always wash your hands thoroughly (preferably using one of the many excellent antibacterial hand soaps) before touching any food intended for your baby. Make sure that all surfaces are clean; ideally, they should be wiped daily using an antibacterial agent such as Dettox. If you have pets, never allow them anywhere near the areas where you prepare your baby's food.

Pay particular attention to the cleanliness of dishcloths, tea towels and chopping boards, all of which can harbour germs. (Plastic or glass chopping boards are preferable to wooden.) Utensils should be washed in hot soapy water and rinsed well, so that no traces of detergent remain. Avoid non-stick pans, as their surfaces have a tendency to 'pit' and trap particles of food, thus creating a potential source of contamination. Aluminium pans should also be avoided as there is some question as to whether the aluminium metal is absorbed by food cooked in such pans. Make sure that your refrigerator is operating at the correct temperature – a purpose-designed thermometer is a good investment.

During the first stage of weaning you should sterilise your baby's spoons and bowls along with his bottles. This is no longer necessary after six months, though bottles and teats used for milk should be sterilised for as long as your baby continues to use them.

Food Preparation

Most vegetables and fruits, except those grown organically, are sprayed with pesticides. As no one can offer any guarantees about the long-term safety of even minute traces of these chemicals, it makes sense to peel all fruit and vegetables. Always cook fruit and vegetables for the minimum possible time to preserve as many nutrients as possible (except pulses and beans which should be boiled rapidly for at least ten minutes to destroy harmful toxins, then cooked until completely tender so that they can be easily digested). To avoid adding fat during the cooking process, choose steaming and microwaving methods in preference to boiling, frying or roasting.

Never add salt to food intended for your baby. Herbs may be used to vary the flavour of a dish and, at the second stage of weaning, a modest amount of spice. For toddlers, alcohol is a perfectly acceptable ingredient, as the alcohol evaporates during cooking, leaving only the flavour.

Frozen Assets

When preparing meals for your baby, you will almost inevitably find that you have a surplus. It's worth freezing this immediately so that you have a stock of foods for those occasions when you have no time to cook. (It is not advisable to store food for babies in the refrigerator for any length of time. If food cannot be frozen, just make enough for immediate use.) Use the freezing symbols at the end of each recipe as a guide to which foods freeze best.

To begin with, ice-cube trays are ideal for freezing baby-sized portions, but, as your baby's appetite increases, clean yoghurt pots or similar-sized containers become more suitable (see Chapter Two). Don't be tempted to stock up for months; your baby's appetite and preferences will change so rapidly during this period that it would be imprudent to plan more than four weeks ahead. Also, while freezing is a good method of preserving food, the nutritional value of frozen food does diminish with time.

The Recipes

All the recipes included in the following chapters are ones which my son has tried and tested and, on occasion (remember, babies' tastes are fickle), enjoyed. The number of portions is given in every case, but these can only be approximate, as appetites vary enormously. I am confident that the recipes introduce children to a wide spectrum of flavours and cuisines while ensuring that they receive at the same time the best possible range of nutrients to aid healthy growth and development. Adapt the recipes to suit your own family's taste, register the reaction in the box provided, and, above all, do enjoy the unique experience of feeding your child.

CHAPTER TWO

First Flavours
FOUR TO SIX MONTHS

Somewhere between the ages of four to six months, most babies will begin to show signs that they are ready for their first taste of real food. To begin with, the amount eaten will be quite literally just a taste, but it is still well worth the time and trouble to prepare home-made fruit and vegetable purées, as the flavours experienced in these early days will determine your baby's food preferences over the coming months and years.

As all new mothers quickly learn, myself included, parental peer-group pressure positively explodes once hitherto sensible individuals produce an offspring on which to foist their thwarted ambitions. The obvious extremes (flash cards at four weeks, analyses of Mozart operas at six months) are easy to dismiss, but when it comes to ordinary milestones like weaning and walking, such pressure can become insidious. I well remember the totally irrational sense of failure I experienced on returning home with my still contentedly breast-fed twelve-week-old son from a routine clinic visit where I had discovered that several babies of the same age had already started on solids. Did this mean my son's development was arrested? What if his growth were stunted?

At this stage, as at every other stage, all babies are individuals who develop at their own pace. Moreover, experts agree that there is no advantage whatsoever in early weaning, but that there are several very real disadvantages. Until your baby is at least four months old, the digestive system is not mature enough to cope with anything other than milk, which contains all the necessary vital nutrients. By introducing solid foods too early you would run the risk of reducing your baby's appetite for the milk he or she needs to grow and thrive, and increasing the chance of stomach upsets and food allergies. While some babies are obviously ready for solids at four months, others continue to gain weight and show no interest in foods other than milk until at least six months. Bottle-fed babies tend to start on solids earlier than breast-fed ones, probably because formula milk does not adapt to your baby's changing requirements as breast milk does.

Let your own baby guide you as to when he or she is ready for solids. Look for the tell-tale indications, such as putting toys and objects in the mouth, demanding feeds at shorter intervals and seeming less satisfied, and showing an interest in your meals (perhaps reaching out for your food).

How to Wean Your Baby

For a baby used to sucking, eating is a new skill that must be mastered. It takes time to get used to the idea. Begin by offering a little solid food just once a day – lunchtime is usually best because then your baby will be most alert. Avoid teatime because, in the unlikely event that a new food disagrees with your baby, you would then both have a disturbed night.

Prepare no more than a tablespoon of tepid rice, or single fruit or vegetable purée (see Basic Purées). Start by giving half the normal breast or bottle feed (otherwise your baby will be too hungry to concentrate on the new experience and you'll both become frustrated), then dip the end of a plastic spoon in the purée. Introduce the spoon between your baby's lips (don't push it in as this causes gagging) and allow him or her to lick the food off. The first spoonful may just be spat out, but don't force things, simply try again. After a few attempts, or when about a teaspoonful has been eaten (the reason for the discrepancy between amount prepared and amount consumed will immediately become apparent!), clean your baby's mouth and resume milk feeding.

For the first two or three weeks offer the same food for at least three days to enable your baby to become accustomed to it and you to monitor reactions. After about three weeks you can increase the amount to about four teaspoons and introduce a little baby rice halfway through the breakfast-time feed. Once your baby is happily taking this amount you can start to introduce a little solid food at teatime, then offer two courses at lunch: a vegetable purée followed by a fruit purée. Within two to three months you should find that your baby is eating solids three times a day and no longer requires a milk feed at lunchtime (to quench thirst, offer boiled cooled water in a beaker).

Good First Foods

Most fruit and vegetables are suitable first foods for babies, although citrus and berry fruits are best avoided at first as they can be too acidic for immature digestive systems. Always wash, peel and cook fruit and vegetables thoroughly (I have indicated in the recipes on the following pages the few instances where this is unnecessary) and purée the flesh to a very smooth consistency. Often you will find that extra liquid is required to make the consistency of the purée acceptable to your baby. This liquid can be boiled water or, preferably, breast or bottle milk. Do not replace breast or formula milk, even in cooking, until your baby

is at least six months old. Note that there are nutritional advantages in continuing longer with such a milk, designed as it is specifically for human babies.

Proteins such as cheese, yoghurt, cream, eggs, pulses and legumes should also be avoided until weaning is firmly established. The gluten-free cereals (that is, rice, millet and maize) may be introduced from the very beginning, but wait until your baby is happily tolerating these (and certainly not before six months) before attempting to introduce wheat and even oats. Avoid porridge oats unless they are very finely ground.

And, however bland these first foods may seem to your sophisticated adult palate, never be tempted to add salt or sugar to food intended for your baby; salt will harm the kidneys and sugar will just educate your baby to expect sweet foods. The natural sweetness of fruit and some vegetables, especially root vegetables, is perfectly adequate.

Equipment

You don't need a great deal of special equipment to prepare food for your baby, but certain items do make the process much simpler. A food processor or mouli-legumes, saves a lot of time and wrist work. Although I already had a food processor, I found a baby version (the sort that's designed for chopping herbs and nuts) absolutely invaluable, as small quantities seem to get lost and process unevenly in a larger bowl. Also, however scrupulous one is about cleaning such dishes, strong flavours such as garlic and chilli do have a tendency to linger. A nylon sieve is also essential for anything with seeds or tough fibres.

If you plan to make batches of baby food (anything over a tablespoon constitutes a batch at this stage), a couple of plastic ice-cube trays are ideal for freezing the surplus. Keep the trays exclusively for baby food and defrost one or two cubes as required.

If you haven't used them before, invest in an adequate supply of plastic-backed bibs to protect your child's clothes – you'll be amazed at just how far one teaspoonful of puréed carrot can spread. (I began weaning my son at about the same time that he learnt to blow raspberries; as a result, our wallpaper featured an interesting multi-coloured textured effect for some time.) If you plan to feed your baby sitting on your lap rather than in a bouncy chair or portable car seat, buy a capacious apron for yourself, too.

Most chemists and baby-equipment stores sell reasonably priced plastic weaning spoons, which have chunky square tips and so are easy for your baby to lick from. A couple of small plastic bowls with handles and suction bases are also a good idea. You'll also need a trainer beaker with a spout. As this will spend a great deal more time horizontal than vertical, ensure that the lid fits securely.

Hygiene

It is especially important to practise good kitchen hygiene when preparing food for young babies, as their delicate digestive systems and low resistance make them especially vulnerable to infection. Wipe kitchen surfaces with an anti-bacterial solution at least once a day and change hand towels, tea towels and dishcloths daily. A dishwasher is the best method of cleaning cooking utensils but, if you don't have one, wash dishes thoroughly in hot soapy water, rinse well and allow to drain until dry. If it is necessary to dry dishes and utensils, use disposable kitchen paper rather than tea towels, which can harbour germs.

Although it is not necessary to sterilise cooking utensils, it is advisable to sterilise your baby's cups, dishes and spoons, at least for the first couple of months. Always discard any food which is left in your baby's dish (bacteria from the spoon may contaminate it) and only ever warm defrosted food once. Wash your hands religiously before preparing food for your baby, and try to get into the habit of washing his or her hands before, as well as after, mealtimes. Grubby little fists make great breeding grounds for all sorts of undesirable bacteria. Stomach upsets are distressing for your baby but even more so for you, so it is worth taking these precautions to prevent problems.

Baby Rice

Most health professionals recommend baby rice as the very first solid food for babies, as it is nutritious, easy to digest and free from gluten. While there are many excellent commercial varieties available, it is easy – and much cheaper – to prepare your own. Many mothers are deterred from doing so by the enticing list of fortifying nutrients on the packets of commercial rice, but at this stage your baby still obtains all the necessary nutrients from milk, so added nutrients are an unnecessary luxury. Always use refined white rice as young babies cannot easily digest brown rice. It's worth keeping a supply of rice in the freezer, as it can be added to any of the purées on the following pages, thus providing extra volume.

MAKES 12–16 PORTIONS

50 g/2 oz short-grain white rice

Wash the rice thoroughly under running water, place in a small saucepan and add sufficient boiling water to cover by approximately 6 mm/¼ in. Stir once, cover with a tight-fitting lid and simmer very gently for 30–40 minutes, until all the water is absorbed and the grains are very tender. Purée with breast or formula milk to a smooth, creamy consistency.

Basic Purées

Simple fruit and vegetable purées are the ideal first foods for your baby As he or she becomes more accustomed to solids you can start to experiment with combinations of fruits and vegetables but, to begin with, it is best to serve them individually. You will then be able to identify the flavours your baby enjoys, those that are likely to be an acquired taste and those that actively disagree with him or her.

The quantities given for the single purées are the smallest that it is feasible to prepare. In the early stages of weaning they may be sufficient for three or four 'meals', but you will soon find that the whole amount disappears at one sitting. This is the time to double or quadruple quantities and freeze the surplus for future use. Where extra liquid is specified, use breast or formula milk for preference, or boiled water.

APPLE

I found that Cox's Orange Pippins were a particularly successful variety for purées.

1 small eating apple

Wash, peel, core and chop the apple. Place in a small saucepan with a little water, bring to the boil and simmer until very tender, about 5–8 minutes. Purée to a smooth consistency, adding extra liquid if necessary.

APRICOT

In the early stages of weaning, try combining apricot purée with baby rice. After banana, this was my son's favourite first food.

3 fresh, ripe apricots

Wash the fruits, skin them and cut in half. Place in a small saucepan with a little water, bring to the boil, cover and simmer until tender, about 10–15 minutes. Purée until smooth, adding extra liquid if necessary.

BANANA

Banana is one of the very few fruits that can safely be given uncooked to babies in the early stages of weaning. However, do be warned that the fruit fibres may at first pass through your baby undigested! Choose a very ripe, unblemished fruit.

½ small banana

Mash the banana with a fork until no lumps remain. Add sufficient breast or formula milk to give a smooth consistency.

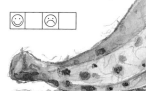

PEAR

Once solid feeding has been established, there is no need to cook ripe pears before puréeing. However, in the initial stages, light cooking does make the fruit easier for your baby to tolerate.

1 *small ripe pear*

Wash, peel and core the pear. Place in a small saucepan with a little water, bring to the boil, cover and simmer until very soft, about 5–8 minutes, depending on the variety of pear. Purée to a smooth consistency, adding extra liquid if necessary.

PEACH

Ripe peaches are a perfect first food for babies: sweet, succulent and very juicy.

1 *small ripe peach*

Wash the peach and remove the skin by scoring a cross in it and submerging the fruit in boiling water for 2–3 minutes. The skin should then lift away with ease. Peel and chop the fruit and place in a small saucepan with a little water, bring to the boil, cover and simmer until tender, about 10 minutes. Purée the cooked peach flesh to a smooth consistency, adding extra liquid if necessary.

PRUNE

Although many adults have an aversion to prunes (perhaps remembering school dinners), babies seem to love them. You may find that they have a laxative effect but I found that this was largely counteracted by mixing them with an equal quantity of baby rice. Later on, try combining prunes with mashed banana.

5 *no-soak stoned prunes*

Wash the prunes thoroughly and place in a small saucepan. Cover with cold water, bring to the boil and simmer for 20–30 minutes, or until very tender. Purée to a smooth consistency, adding extra liquid if necessary.

MANGO

Use the small, yellow Indian Alphonso mangoes (from Asian supermarkets and greengrocers) rather than the larger, green African ones which are more widely available. Although the Alphonso mangoes are only briefly in season, their milder, sweeter flavour is perfect for babies.

1 *small mango*

Scrub the mango thoroughly and peel. Cut the flesh away from the stone. Purée to a smooth consistency.

MELON

Any variety of melon can be given uncooked to a baby, provided that the melon is very ripe and the skin is well washed before you cut into it. However, I think that Galia melons tend to be sweeter than other varieties. If the fruit is not entirely ripe, steam it lightly before puréeing.

1 *small wedge of melon*

Cut the melon flesh away from the skin, removing all of the slightly greener fruit close to the skin. Purée to a smooth consistency. Because melons contain a high proportion of water it should not be necessary to add extra liquid.

MARROW

Marrow is both bland in flavour and easy to digest, making it an ideal first food. Avoid very large specimens as, despite their prize-winning potential at local produce shows, these can prove dry and fibrous.

1 *thick slice of marrow*

Peel the marrow and cut out the seeds and pith. Chop the flesh into cubes and steam it over boiling water for 10–15 minutes, or until tender. Mash the flesh with a fork until smooth.

CARROT

Carrots seems universally popular with young babies, probably because of their natural sweetness. Use young, tender specimens as these tend to be less fibrous.

1 *medium carrot*

Scrub the carrot thoroughly, cut off the tip and root, and peel. Place in a pan of lightly boiling water, cover and simmer for about 30 minutes or until very tender. Drain, reserving the cooking liquid, and purée to a smooth consistency, adding as much of the reserved liquid as necessary.

AVOCADO

Avocados are highly nutritious, and their lovely creamy texture and bland taste are ideal for babies. They also have the advantage of being one of the few 'instant' foods you can offer a young baby. Choose a soft, ripe fruit and prepare avocado immediately before your baby is due to eat, in order to prevent the flesh discolouring.

1 *slice medium-ripe avocado*

Mash the flesh (using a fork) or purée, adding breast or formula milk to give the desired consistency.

POTATO

For young babies, old, floury varieties of potato are best, as they 'fall' when cooked and so mash better. Choose a specimen with as smooth and unblemished a skin as possible.

1 medium potato

Scrub the potato, peel, and cut out any blemishes. Cut the potato into evenly sized chunks. Place in a saucepan of boiling water, cover and simmer until very tender, about 20–30 minutes. Drain and mash (using a fork) to a smooth consistency, adding breast or formula milk if extra liquid is required.

SWEET POTATO

The creamy orange flesh of this exotic cousin to our native potato appeals especially to babies. You could boil sweet potato as above, but I prefer to bake it.

1 small sweet potato

Scrub the potato skin, dry it and prick all over with a fork. Bake at 400°F (200°C) Gas Mark 6 for ¾–1 hour, or until soft. Split the skin, scoop out the flesh and mash (using a fork) to a smooth consistency, adding breast or formula milk.

PARSNIP

In common with other root vegetables, parsnip has a natural sweetness which immediately appeals to babies' palates. Choose small, young parsnips which have the best flavour and texture.

1 medium parsnip

Scrub the parsnip, trim away the root and tip, and cut into quarters lengthways. Cut away the woody central core and chop the parsnip into evenly sized pieces. Place in a saucepan of boiling water, cover and simmer for 25–30 minutes, or until very tender. Purée to a smooth consistency, adding extra liquid if necessary.

CAULIFLOWER

In the early stages of weaning, make sure that cauliflower is very well cooked, otherwise it can give your baby uncomfortable wind.

3–4 cauliflower florets

Wash the cauliflower well. Place it in a saucepan of boiling water, cover and simmer for 10–15 minutes, or until very tender (insert the point of a sharp knife into the stalks to test). Drain and purée to a smooth consistency, adding extra liquid if necessary.

GREEN BEAN

French beans are best for this purée, as they tend to be less stringy than other varieties. If you are unable to obtain French beans, substitute runner beans, in which case you will need to sieve the purée before serving.

5 crisp French beans

Wash the beans thoroughly, then top and tail. Steam them for 10–15 minutes, or until tender and almost wilted. Purée until smooth, adding extra liquid as necessary.

CAULIFLOWER & BROCCOLI

Cauliflower and broccoli have a natural affinity and together produce a pretty green purée which is as harmonious on the eye as it is on the palate.

MAKES 6 PORTIONS

3–4 cauliflower florets
3–4 broccoli florets

Wash the vegetables well. Place them in a saucepan of boiling water, cover and simmer for 10–15 minutes, until the point of a sharp knife can be inserted easily into the stalks. Drain and purée, adding extra liquid as necessary.

CARROT, PARSNIP & SWEDE

As most babies love root vegetables, this falls into the rare 'fail-safe' category.

MAKES 8 PORTIONS

1 medium carrot, scrubbed, peeled and diced
1 medium parsnip, scrubbed, peeled and diced
1 slice swede, peeled and diced

Place the prepared vegetables in a saucepan of boiling water, cover and simmer for approximately 25–30 minutes (depending on the age of the vegetables) until very tender. Drain and purée to a smooth consistency, adding extra liquid as necessary.

GREEN BEAN & RED PEPPER

The natural sweetness of red peppers makes beans more interesting.

MAKES 6 PORTIONS

5 French beans, washed, trimmed and chopped
½ red pepper, washed, seeded and chopped

Place the beans in a saucepan of boiling water, cover and simmer for 5 minutes. Add the chopped pepper and simmer for a further 5 minutes. Drain and purée, adding extra liquid as necessary.

POTATO, LEEK & SPINACH

The taste of onion can be a little overpowering for babies, and its effect on immature digestive systems can be dramatic. Leek is a subtler alternative.

MAKES 10 PORTIONS

1 *medium potato, scrubbed, peeled and diced*
1 *tender young leek, thoroughly washed,*
trimmed and chopped
5 *fresh spinach leaves, washed, stalks*
removed and chopped

Place the potato and leek in a saucepan of boiling water, cover and simmer until very tender, about 20 minutes. Drain. Meanwhile, place the prepared spinach leaves (with the water adhering to them after washing) in another saucepan over a gentle heat. Simmer gently for 10–15 minutes, or until tender. Drain and purée with the potato and leek, adding extra liquid as necessary.

CELERIAC & POTATO

This makes a delicious purée, which is loved just as much by adults.

MAKES 8 PORTIONS

1 *thick slice celeriac, scrubbed, peeled and chopped*
1 *medium potato, scrubbed, peeled and chopped*

Place the celeriac and potato in a saucepan of boiling water, cover and simmer until tender, about 20–30 minutes. Drain and mash to a smooth purée (using a fork), adding sufficient breast or formula milk to give the required consistency.

COURGETTE & CARROT

Combining carrots with courgettes made me feel better about serving them so frequently!

MAKES 8 PORTIONS

1 *medium carrot, scrubbed, peeled, topped and tailed*
1 *small courgette, washed and trimmed*

Dice the carrot and courgette. Add the diced carrot to a saucepan of boiling water, cover and simmer for about 15 minutes. Add the courgette and continue cooking for a further 10–15 minutes. Drain the vegetables and purée to a smooth consistency. The courgettes are very watery, so you should not need to add extra liquid.

PARSNIP & APPLE

Fruit and vegetable combinations often work; but this is especially successful.

MAKES 8 PORTIONS

1 small young parsnip
1 small eating apple

Scrub, top and tail, and peel the parsnip. Cut into quarters, core and dice. Wash, peel, core and chop the apple. Place the parsnip pieces in a saucepan of boiling water, cover and simmer for 15 minutes, add the apple and continue cooking for a further 5–10 minutes. Drain and purée to a smooth consistency, adding extra liquid as necessary.

APPLE & PEAR

Another 'fail-safe' combination, this makes a great freezer standby.

MAKES 6–8 PORTIONS

1 small eating apple, washed, peeled,
cored and chopped
1 small ripe pear, washed, peeled, cored and chopped

Place the fruit in a saucepan with a little water. Bring to the boil, cover and simmer for 5–8 minutes or until tender. Purée to a smooth consistency, adding extra liquid as necessary.

PRUNE & APPLE

This preserves the flavour of the prunes, while counteracting their side effects.

MAKES 8–10 PORTIONS

Mix together 1 quantity apple purée and 1 quantity prune purée (see pages 23–4).

APRICOT & PEACH

Not so much a purée, more a nectar.

MAKES 8 PORTIONS

Mix together 1 quantity apricot and 1 quantity peach purée (see pages 23–4). For slightly older babies, add a little fromage frais (use the type with 10 per cent fat).

AVOCADO & PEAR

The sweet/savoury contrast makes this combination very successful.

MAKES 1 PORTION

1 slice ripe avocado
1 slice very ripe pear, peeled

Mash the avocado and pear together until smooth and well combined. For older babies, add a little cottage cheese to the mixture for added protein.

FOUR TO SIX MONTHS MENU CHART

Use this Menu Chart as a guide only. You can substitute any of the purée recipes for those suggested here, so long as you introduce one food at a time, and let your baby dictate the pace.

INGREDIENTS CHECKLIST *

Apples
Carrots
Rice

Week 1&2	Early Morning	Breakfast	Lunch	Tea	Bedtime
Day 1	Milk	Milk	Milk Baby Rice	Milk	Milk
Day 2	Milk	Milk	Milk Baby Rice	Milk	Milk
Day 3	Milk	Milk	Milk Baby Rice	Milk	Milk
Day 4	Milk	Milk	Milk Apple Purée	Milk	Milk
Day 5	Milk	Milk	Milk Apple Purée	Milk	Milk
Day 6	Milk	Milk	Milk Apple Purée	Milk	Milk
Day 7	Milk	Milk	Milk Carrot Purée	Milk	Milk

NB In this and subsequent Menu Charts, recipes contained in this book are indicated in bold type.

* Use this Ingredients Checklist and those in later chapters to help you shop, depending on the preferences of your baby and how closely you decide to follow the menu charts (basic store-cupboard ingredients are not included).

FOUR TO SIX MONTHS MENU CHART *cont.*

After a week or so, your baby will be ready to progress to two solid feeds a day and you can begin to vary the diet from day to day.

INGREDIENTS CHECKLIST

Avocado
Bananas
Marrow
Parsnips
Peaches
Pears
Potatoes
Rice

Week 3	Early Morning	Breakfast	Lunch	Tea	Bedtime
Day 1	Milk	Milk Baby Rice	Milk Marrow Purée	Milk	Milk
Day 2	Milk	Milk Baby Rice	Milk Pear Purée	Milk	Milk
Day 3	Milk	Milk Baby Rice	Milk Potato Purée	Milk	Milk
Day 4	Milk	Milk Baby Rice	Milk Mashed Banana	Milk	Milk
Day 5	Milk	Milk Baby Rice	Milk Parsnip Purée	Milk	Milk
Day 6	Milk	Milk Baby Rice	Milk Peach Purée	Milk	Milk
Day 7	Milk	Milk Baby Rice	Milk Mashed Avocado	Milk	Milk

FOUR TO SIX MONTHS MENU CHART *cont.*

Towards the end of the first month of weaning, your baby will be ready for three 'meals' a day, though of course these will still be just small tasters.

INGREDIENTS CHECKLIST

Apples
Apricots
Avocado
Bananas
Carrots
Cauliflower
French beans
Mango
Melon
Pears
Potatoes
Prunes
Rice
Sweet potato

Week 4	Early Morning	Breakfast	Lunch	Tea	Bedtime
Day 1	Milk	Milk Baby Rice	Sweet Potato Purée Milk	Apricot Purée Milk	Milk
Day 2	Milk	Milk Baby Rice	Cauliflower Purée Milk	Prune Purée Milk	Milk
Day 3	Milk	Milk Baby Rice	Green Bean Purée Milk	Melon Purée Milk	Milk
Day 4	Milk	Milk Baby Rice	Carrot Purée Pear Purée Water Milk	Mashed Banana Milk	Milk
Day 5	Milk	Milk Baby Rice	Potato Purée Prune Purée Water Milk	Apple Purée Milk	Milk
Day 6	Milk	Milk Baby Rice	Cauliflower Purée Pear Purée Water Milk	Mango Purée Milk	Milk
Day 7	Milk	Milk Baby Rice	Avocado Purée Melon Purée Water Milk	Mashed Banana Milk	Milk

FOUR TO SIX MONTHS MENU CHART *cont.*

Your baby's appetite for solids and larger quantities should now be firmly established. You may now safely combine fruits and vegetables to make more interesting purées.

INGREDIENTS CHECKLIST

Apples
Apricots
Avocado
Baby cereal
Bananas
Broccoli
Carrots
Cauliflower
Celeriac
Courgettes
French beans
Leeks
Mango
Marrow
Melon
Parsnips
Peas
Peaches
Pears
Potatoes
Prunes
Red pepper
Spinach
Swede

Week 5&6	Early Morning	Breakfast	Lunch	Tea	Bedtime
Day 1	Milk	Mashed Banana Milk	Carrot, Parsnip & Swede Purée Melon Purée Boiled water	Mashed Avocado Milk	Milk
Day 2	Milk	Baby cereal Milk	Celeriac & Potato Purée Prune Purée Boiled water	Mashed Banana Milk	Milk
Day 3	Milk	Apple & Pear Purée Milk	Cauliflower & Broccoli Purée Peach Purée Boiled water	Marrow Purée Milk	Milk
Day 4	Milk	Baby cereal Milk	Pea & Leek Purée Apricot Purée Boiled water	Prune & Apple Purée Milk	Milk
Day 5	Milk	Mashed Banana Milk	Potato & Spinach Purée Apple & Pear Purée Boiled water	Carrot Purée Milk	Milk
Day 6	Milk	Baby cereal Milk	Green Bean & Red Pepper Purée Prune Purée Boiled water	Peach Purée Milk	Milk
Day 7	Milk	Mango Purée Milk	Courgette & Carrot Purée Banana	Avocado & Pear Purée Milk	Milk

CHAPTER THREE

Texture & Taste

SIX TO NINE MONTHS

Somewhere between the ages of six and nine months, most babies will enter what experts and health professionals term the second stage of weaning. Broadly speaking this means the stage at which they are able to tolerate proteins (other than milk) and gluten and cope with some texture in their food. This can be the beginning of a short honeymoon phase when it comes to feeding your child (though some do become fussy at this time). Over the next few months your baby will probably establish a fairly regular eating pattern, gain weight rapidly, enjoy something approximating three meals a day and display very few feeding fads. Though most babies are more than content with a fairly monotonous diet, make the most of this phase while it lasts to introduce as many new flavours and textures as possible. You'll be doing both yourself and your child a great service in the long term.

At this age, milk still plays a major role in your baby's diet, but milk alone is no longer nutritionally adequate. The iron stores that your baby is born with are depleting and the rapid growth rate means that extra protein, vitamins, minerals and calories are all required. From now onwards, for the next year or so at least, you should still ensure that your baby has at least 600 ml/1 pint of milk a day in addition to solid food. This amount of milk is necessary for the continued healthy development of bones and teeth.

Whether you give breast or formula milk is entirely a matter of personal choice, although cow's milk should not be introduced (other than in cooking) until your baby is at least one year old. If you have breast-fed your baby during the first few months and now for reasons of convenience (perhaps because of a return to work) you decide to opt for bottles instead, there is no need to feel guilty. The major advantages of breast feeding are already confirmed, such as increased resistance to disease as a result of receiving maternal antibodies. Some mothers find that they can happily continue feeding at bedtime only for an indefinite time, so, if this suits you and your baby, by all means continue. Personally, I found that once I switched to bottles during the day my milk supply rapidly dried up.

Once solid feeding is well established do not offer your baby milk to drink at mealtimes, as this tends to detract from his or her appetite and makes for a cross, hungry baby a short while later. Instead of milk, offer very weak fruit juice or, preferably, boiled water to quench thirst. Always give your baby juice in a feeder cup or beaker, never a bottle. Although the sugars naturally present in fruit juice are nutritionally preferable to artificial sugars, your baby's delicate new teeth unfortunately can't tell the difference (and it is now thought that the acids in many commercial drinks and fruit juices are also very harmful to teeth). And don't be seduced into believing that many of the commercial herbal drinks available are any less harmful. Ignore the hype, read the label and reject anything with a high proportion of 'oses', that is, fructose, sucrose and lactose, which are just sugar in scientific clothing. Avoid artificial sweeteners such as saccharine and aspartame, found in sugar-free squashes and some yoghurts (they are banned from being added to baby foods).

TOWARDS THREE MEALS

Once your baby has got to grips with solid food you will find that he or she soon learns to enjoy regular mealtimes. Now that gluten (found in wheat products like bread and cereals) is no longer a problem, cereals together with some form of fruit are an excellent choice for breakfast. Despite the marketing pressure on parents to purchase special baby cereals, a bag of porridge oats, preferably organic, and a box of wholewheat biscuits are all you need to ensure a healthy start to your baby's day.

At this age it is best to make lunch the main meal of the day and this is also the time to introduce new foods. Your baby is more likely to be receptive in the middle of the day and, in the unlikely event of one food having a disagreeable effect, there is time to deal with the consequences before bedtime.

And, while on this subject, it is worth mentioning that much of what goes in will come out in a recognisable form. (I offer this reassurance so that you do not repeat my experience of rushing my baby and his alarming nappy to casualty, to be greeted by hoots of derision.)

Remember, too, that appetite can exceed ability at this age. When my son Krishnan was nine months old, we spent a holiday in France and were delighted to be able to take him out to restaurants with us in the evenings where he would happily suck on a hunk of baguette while we enjoyed dinner. After several days he began to refuse food and we subsequently discovered a huge wad of pulped bread welded to the roof of his mouth! In other words, babies will, quite literally, bite off more than they can chew. For this reason, they should never be left unattended while eating.

GENERAL GUIDELINES

Most fruits and vegetables are now acceptable but they should still be washed thoroughly, peeled, and, where appropriate (e.g. grapes, tomatoes), seeded. Wheat-based foods such as bread and cereal may be given freely. You may now also introduce cheese and eggs, but avoid soft and blue cheeses, and use only the yolks of eggs, as egg white is still difficult for your baby to digest. Eggs must be hard boiled to kill any salmonella or other bacteria. Introduce

pulses as an alternative source of protein, but make the process gradual, and mash them or they will pass through undigested. Mash beans or lentils with a little oil to make them more palatable and add essential calories.

Never be afraid to add a good-quality vegetable oil, such as olive oil, soya oil or walnut oil, to home-prepared baby foods. This applies particularly to vegetarian babies who are not consuming fat in animal foods.

You can, and should, begin to introduce moderate amounts of herbs and spices as flavourings at this stage, and I recommend this wherever possible if you don't wish to be landed with a fussy toddler who views every unidentified fleck with suspicion. The only absolute seasoning no-go area is salt. Until your baby is at least one year old the kidneys will be too immature to deal with it. As many of the recipes which follow are suitable for the whole family, I suggest that you isolate your baby's portion before seasoning your own.

TEXTURE

In the parental interests of trouble-free, fast feeding, it is all too tempting to continue puréeing your baby's food to a spoonable mush indefinitely. In a word, don't, or you will end up with one of those infuriating infants who rejects every piece of fruit in yoghurt and lines up on the side of the plate every chunk of vegetable more than a few millimetres square. Begin by mashing rather than puréeing food and don't worry if at first your baby gags and spits a little. Babies quickly get the hang of chewing, even if they don't have many, or any, teeth. Gums are remarkably efficient at pulverising well-cooked vegetables. Toast soldiers, rusks, cubes of cheese and crudités are all ideal ways of introducing your child to interesting textures and the mechanics of mastication.

QUANTITIES

Each recipe in this book gives the number of portions produced, but this is always approximate. Each individual baby's appetite is the only infallible guide to quantity. I have come across babies built like small sumo wrestlers who happily toy with a couple of teaspoons of food at every meal and continue to thrive. My own son, who has remained on the lower weight centile since birth, used to, and still does, consume alarming quantities of food. I am only sorry to report that he has not inherited his remarkable metabolism from the maternal side. My advice is to offer your baby a little to begin with, and keep going until interest seems to have waned. Provided your baby continues to gain weight and make good progress, you can rest assured that all is well.

PRACTICALITIES

Make sure your baby is comfortable before attempting to feed. At around six months, most babies are taking their meals in a bouncy chair or on your lap; towards the end of this phase they have usually progressed to a high chair. Try to ensure a calm, relaxed atmosphere and never force your baby to eat. Like you, sometimes he or she will be genuinely hungry, but at other times food may not be needed. Never serve a baby hot food; always cool it to tepid. If you use a microwave to reheat your baby's food, always leave the food to stand for a minute or so, and check the temperature in the centre (the outside can be scalding while the inside remains cool). Most babies seem to prefer the feel of plastic rather than metal spoons in their mouths and, of course, everything tastes better sucked from their own fists. Pelican bibs are practical, but some children, my own son included, find their rigidity claustrophobic. In this case, try compromising with a laminated cotton bib. Above all, try to make feeding your baby a special time to share rather than a chore.

SOUPS AND DIPS

Parsnip & Apple Soup

Fruit and root combinations readily appeal to palates still attuned to the natural sweetness of breast milk. To make a thicker, more substantial purée, simply reduce the amount of vegetable stock and milk.

MAKES 12 PORTIONS

25 g/1 oz butter
750 g/1½ lb parsnips, peeled and
roughly chopped
1 large cooking apple, peeled, cored and
roughly chopped

pinch of dried sage (optional)
1 litre/1½ pints unsalted
vegetable stock
150 ml/5 fl oz fromage frais

Melt the butter and gently fry the parsnips and apple for 10 minutes, or until soft. Sprinkle the sage (if using) on to the parsnips and apple, and stir in the stock. Bring to the boil and simmer for 30–40 minutes, or until the vegetables are very tender. Allow the soup to cool slightly, liquidise, then return to the pan, add the fromage frais and reheat gently.

Ten-minute Tomato Soup

Most children's love affair with tomato soup begins in babyhood, so this quicker-than-opening-a-can version is a great standby. My son has adored this since he was tiny and it is still his best 'poorly food', slipping down a sore throat when all else fails to tempt. For healthy infants, try serving with fingers of dry toast or breadsticks which they can dip into the soup themselves while you take charge of the spoon.

MAKES 12 PORTIONS

250 ml/8 fl oz passata   mixture of milk and single cream
600 ml/1 pint milk, or   pinch of sugar, or to taste

Heat the passata gently, stir in the milk, or milk and cream mixture, bring to the boil and allow to simmer gently for 5 minutes. Add a little sugar to taste.

Crudités

Crudités are a good way of introducing your baby to raw foods and encouraging the idea of chewing as a useful aid to eating, rather than just a means of exploration! Although at this age very little of the vegetables will actually be consumed, they will ease the soreness of teething gums while helping to develop your child's burgeoning sense of independence, and feeding skills.

Celery   Green beans, lightly steamed
Carrot   Mangetout, lightly steamed
Florets of cauliflower and broccoli,   Baby ears of corn, lightly steamed
lightly steamed   Avocado slices

Vegetables served in this way should be washed thoroughly, peeled and cut into manageable pieces, small enough for tiny fists to grip, yet large enough to prevent your baby swallowing them whole and choking. I have found that the varieties above are particularly well-received. Serve them with a nutritious dip (see the suggestions on the following pages) for a tasty teatime treat.

Avocado & Cottage Cheese Dip

Babies love the creamy, smooth texture of avocado as well as its unchallenging taste. Make this dip as close to mealtime as possible, as the avocado flesh will discolour. If you have to prepare it in advance, placing the stone in the bowl helps to prevent discoloration. The recipe gives enough to make an adult dip as well – just add seasoning and a dash of tabasco sauce.

MAKES 4–6 PORTIONS

1 *medium-sized, ripe avocado*   100 *g/4 oz cottage cheese*

Cut the avocado in half, remove the stone, and place the flesh in the bowl of a food processor. Add the cottage cheese. Blend until smooth.

Happy Hummus

Commercially prepared hummus contains a great deal of salt, which is undesirable for young babies. This version retains all the goodness without the unwanted extra salt.

MAKES 6 PORTIONS

400 *g/14 oz can chickpeas, drained*   60 *ml/4 tablespoons tahini*
and rinsed   *(sesame-seed paste)*
½ *clove garlic, crushed*   *juice of ½ lemon*
                                               a little Greek yoghurt

Place the chickpeas, garlic, tahini and lemon juice in the bowl of a food processor. Blend until smooth, adding a little Greek yoghurt to the mixture to achieve the required consistency.

Creamy Cheese Dip

Mild and mollifying, this simple savoury is especially enjoyable with chunks of apple, pineapple or pear to plunge into it.

MAKES 4 PORTIONS

50 g /2 oz red Leicester cheese, grated
25 g/1 oz natural yoghurt

15 g/½ oz softened butter

Place the grated cheese, yoghurt and softened butter in a bowl. Beat together until smooth and creamy.

Magic Mushroom Mush

I call this magic not because it incorporates hallucinogenic fungi (though at the end of a trying day mothers may well wish it did), but because many small children have an in-built aversion to mushrooms, and, prepared in this way, they seem to become magically acceptable. Try this as a sandwich filling as well as a dip.

MAKES 8–10 PORTIONS

15 ml/1 tablespoon olive oil
1 small onion, finely chopped
225 g/8 oz mushrooms, wiped and finely chopped

½ clove garlic, peeled and crushed
2 tablespoons finely chopped parsley
350 g/12 oz canned cannellini beans, drained and rinsed

Heat the oil and gently fry the onion until soft, about 10 minutes. Add the mushrooms, garlic and parsley and continue to cook for about 15 minutes, until soft. Place the cooked vegetables in the bowl of a food processor, together with the cannellini beans, and blend until smooth. Chill before using.

SANDWICHES

Tiny sandwiches make great finger food (think doll's house steps rather than doorstops). At this age, like most babies, Krishnan preferred white bread to brown and, though white bread has a lower fibre content, on a vegetarian diet this is not a problem. The following filling suggestions were his teatime favourites.

Grated Cheese with Pear
& Apple Spread

Pear and apple spread is available from most health food shops. Because it is made entirely from concentrated fruit juice it has the sweetness which babies love without the added sugar.

MAKES 2 SANDWICHES OR MORE FINGERS

2 *thin slices white bread*
1 *teaspoon softened butter*

1 *teaspoon pear and apple spread*
25 *g/1 oz mild Cheddar cheese, grated*

Spread the bread sparingly with butter, then the pear and apple spread. Top one slice with grated cheese, sandwich together and cut into small fingers.

Cream Cheese & Pineapple

Use full-fat cream cheese for babies, as calorie requirements outweigh cholesterol concerns at this age. Vary this combination by replacing the pineapple with peeled, chopped peaches or mashed banana.

MAKES 2 SANDWICHES OR MORE FINGERS

15 ml/1 *tablespoon cream cheese*   2 *thin slices white bread*
1 *slice fresh pineapple, peeled and cored*

P lace the cream cheese and pineapple in the bowl of a food processor and blend until smooth. Spread the bread with this mixture, sandwich together, then cut into quarters or fingers, or use a cocktail pastry cutter to stamp out interesting shapes.

Egg & Cress

Egg white is unsuitable for babies of this age as the proteins it contains are too complex for their digestive systems, but the yolk is a valuable source of both digestible protein and energy. Use the mild, commercial cress, as traditional mustard and cress is a little astringent for babies' palates.

MAKES 2 SANDWICHES OR MORE FINGERS/SHAPES

2 thin slices white bread
1 teaspoon softened butter
1 free-range egg

15 ml/1 tablespoon Greek yoghurt
¼ carton cress, chopped

Spread the bread with the softened butter. Boil the egg for 10 minutes, drain and cover with cold water. Peel the egg, discard the shell and egg white, and mash the yolk with the yoghurt. Spread the egg and yoghurt mixture on to the bread, sprinkle the cress over the top and sandwich the bread together. Cut the sandwiches into shapes.

Pink Panther Spread

This deliciously creamy mixture has a lovely delicate pink hue which babies find appealing. The recipe gives enough to make the extra into a spread for adults – just add seasoning and mustard.

MAKES 2 SANDWICHES OR MORE FINGERS/SHAPES

200 g/7 oz can butterbeans,
drained and rinsed
2 tomatoes

2 thin slices white bread
1 teaspoon softened butter

Place the drained butterbeans in the bowl of a food processor. Skin the tomatoes (to make this easier, make an incision in the shape of a cross on the top of the tomato and plunge into boiling water for 2 minutes). Remove the tomato seeds using a pointed teaspoon, and chop the flesh. Add the tomato to the butterbeans and blend to a smooth purée. Spread the butter on the bread then spoon the butter bean and tomato mixture on the bread and sandwich together. Cut the sandwiches into shapes.

Rusks

All babies love to gnaw on rusks, which also make a good breakfast cereal if crumbled into breast or formula milk. Making your own rusks is actually very easy and highly rewarding because they taste so much better (and usually have less sugar) than commercial varieties.

MAKES 36 RUSKS

450 g/1 lb strong white flour
10 ml/2 teaspoons cream of tartar
5 ml/1 teaspoon bicarbonate of soda
75 g/3 oz caster sugar

100 g/4 oz butter
1 free-range egg, beaten
250 ml/8 fl oz buttermilk

Sift the flour, cream of tartar and bicarbonate of soda together. Stir in the sugar. Rub in the butter until the mixture resembles fine breadcrumbs.

Mix together the egg and buttermilk, then add this to the flour mixture and knead lightly until the mixture forms a soft ball. Using your hands, pat the dough evenly into an oiled 33 x 20 cm (13 x 8 in) Swiss roll tin. Mark into 36 fingers using a sharp knife and bake at 400°F (200°C) Gas Mark 6 for 30 minutes. Remove the rusks from the oven, cut into them into slices and arrange them on baking trays. Lower the heat to 250°F (120°C) Gas Mark ½ and return the rusks to the oven until dry. When cool, store the rusks in an airtight container.

French Toast

In our house, any pretensions to gracious living are relentlessly quashed by my four-year-old who persists in referring to one of his favourite baby breakfasts as 'eggy bread'. Nowadays he enjoys it with tomato ketchup, but then, with a mindful eye to salt and sugar levels, I used to serve it with tomato purée.

MAKES 2 PORTIONS

1 *thick slice white bread*
1 *free-range egg, beaten*

a little butter for frying

Beat the egg and pour it into a shallow dish. Soak both sides of the bread in the egg. Heat the butter in a small frying pan and gently fry the egg-soaked bread on both sides until golden and crispy. Slice into fingers.

SUBSTANTIAL SAVOURIES

Macaroni Cheese

As a baby, my son enjoyed macaroni cheese so much, he would, if allowed, have eaten it practically every day. To ring the changes, try adding a few frozen peas and/or some sweetcorn to the cheese sauce.

MAKES 10 PORTIONS

75 g/3 oz macaroni
25 g/1 oz butter
25 g/1 oz plain flour

300 ml/½ pint milk
75 g/3 oz mild Cheddar cheese, grated
15 ml/1 tablespoon dried breadcrumbs

Cook the macaroni according to the directions on the packet. Drain. Melt the butter in a pan, add the flour and cook without colouring for 2 minutes. Using a balloon whisk, gradually incorporate the milk into the flour/butter mixture until you have a smooth sauce. Simmer the sauce for a couple of minutes, then remove from the heat and stir in two-thirds of the grated cheese.

Stir the cooked macaroni into the cheese sauce until it is well coated and transfer to a shallow gratin dish. Mix the remaining cheese with the breadcrumbs, sprinkle it over the macaroni, and place under a preheated grill until golden brown and bubbling.

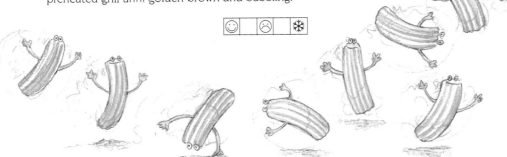

Napolitana Pasta Sauce

This quick, simple-to-make sauce can be used as the basis for many dishes. You can ring the changes by adding vegetables and/or cheese, according to your baby's preferences, or, instead of serving it with pasta, try it on potato gnocchi.

MAKES 6 PORTIONS

10 ml/2 teaspoons olive oil
½ clove garlic, peeled and crushed
10 ml/2 teaspoons chopped fresh basil

10 ml/2 teaspoons chopped fresh
flat-leaf parsley
350 g/12 oz canned chopped tomatoes

Heat the oil, add the garlic and herbs and sauté lightly for 2 minutes. Stir in the tomatoes and simmer, uncovered, for about 15 minutes, until the sauce is reduced and thickened (continue stirring to break up the tomato). Serve with pasta shapes.

Hummus Pasta Sauce

This takes only minutes to prepare, so it is ideal for those frequent occasions when time is at a premium.

MAKES 6 PORTIONS

10 ml/2 teaspoons olive oil
2 spring onions, finely chopped

60 ml/4 tablespoons hummus
(see page 40)
15–30 ml/1–2 tablespoons milk

Heat the oil in a saucepan and gently sauté the onions until soft and golden. Add the hummus and sufficient milk to give a smooth, sauce-like consistency. Simmer gently for 5–10 minutes and serve with tiny pasta shapes.

Sweet Pepper Pasta Sauce

Red peppers are extremely rich in vitamin C, which helps the iron in the parsley to be absorbed by the body. Fortunately, this sauce tastes good too!

MAKES 6 PORTIONS

10 ml/2 teaspoons olive oil
2 red peppers, seeded and chopped
½ small onion, peeled and chopped
¼ clove garlic, finely chopped

60 ml/4 tablespoons canned chopped tomatoes
10 ml/2 teaspoons chopped parsley
pinch of sugar

Heat the oil, add the peppers, onion, garlic and tomatoes and stew gently for 15–20 minutes or until very tender. Stir in the parsley and season with the sugar. Cook for a further 2–3 minutes. Blend to a smooth sauce in a food processor.

Fruity Couscous

Remember to wash the dried fruit thoroughly before using, as most brands are coated in a potentially harmful mineral oil to keep them moist.

MAKES 10 PORTIONS

50 g/2 oz no-soak dried apricots
50 g/2 oz raisins
25 g/1 oz creamed coconut, grated

1 tablespoon raw cane sugar
½ teaspoon cinnamon
100 g/4 oz couscous

Chop the apricots and place in a saucepan with the raisins, adding sufficient water to cover. Bring to the boil and simmer for about 10 minutes, or until tender. Mix the coconut with the sugar and cinnamon and add 300 ml/½ pint water. Transfer the coconut mixture to a saucepan and gradually bring to the boil, stirring, until the coconut flakes and sugar are dissolved. Stir the couscous into the coconut, remove from the heat and cover. Leave to stand for 3–5 minutes, until all the water is absorbed. Fluff up the couscous using a fork. Drain the dried fruit and stir it into the couscous.

☺ ☹ ❄

Khichri

My son's father is from the Indian State of Gujarat where this dish is a staple infant food. True to his genetic heritage, Krishnan loved it from his first spoonful.

MAKES 10 PORTIONS

50 g/2 oz split red lentils
sliver of garlic
sliver of root ginger, peeled
½ bay leaf

1 tomato, skinned, seeded and finely chopped
50 g/2 oz basmati rice
15–30 ml/1–2 tablespoons natural yoghurt

Thoroughly wash and pick over the lentils. Place in a saucepan with the garlic, ginger and bay leaf, cover with water, bring to the boil and simmer for 40–50 minutes or until very tender, adding extra water if required (the cooked lentils should be the consistency of a thick soup). Discard the ginger, garlic and bay leaf. Add the chopped tomato and continue cooking for 5 minutes.

Meanwhile, wash the rice under plenty of running water and cook according to the directions on the packet, until tender. Drain. Combine the rice with the lentil mixture and stir in the yoghurt. For younger babies, purée the mixture.

Spring Vegetable Risotto

Rice is always popular with babies, and the lovely bright greens of the vegetables in this dish are very appealing to small eyes.

MAKES 6–8 PORTIONS

225 g/8 oz mixed green vegetables, e.g.
young peas, courgettes, broad beans
5 ml/1 teaspoon olive oil
knob of butter

3 spring onions, finely chopped
150 g/5 oz arborio rice
500 ml/16 fl oz vegetable stock
½ teaspoon dried oregano

Prepare the green vegetables and steam them for 8–10 minutes, or until tender. Heat the oil and butter gently, add the spring onions and cook until soft. Add the rice to the onions and stir well. Continue frying gently until the rice is opaque but not browned.

Add about a third of the stock to the rice and continue cooking over a low heat until the stock is absorbed, about 10 minutes. Now add another third of the stock, together with the cooked vegetables and oregano and continue cooking until this is also absorbed. Add the remaining stock and allow the rice to continue cooking until it is quite tender and all the liquid has been absorbed. For younger babies, purée the mixture before serving.

Broccoli & Cauliflower Cheese

This is a colourful variation on the perennially popular cauliflower cheese. For a more substantial dish, add a handful of cooked pasta shapes to the sauce with the vegetables.

MAKES 12 PORTIONS

175 g /6 oz cauliflower florets
175 g/6 oz broccoli florets
CHEESE SAUCE
25 g/1 oz butter

30 ml/2 tablespoons plain flour
300 ml/½ pint milk
100 g/4 oz mild Cheddar or Gruyère
cheese, grated

Wash the vegetables and steam until tender but not watery (about 10 minutes). Meanwhile, prepare the cheese sauce; melt the butter, stir in the flour and cook over a low heat for 1–2 minutes, stirring constantly. Gradually whisk in the milk and continue whisking until the sauce is thickened. Remove from the heat, stir in the grated cheese and add the vegetables. Purée in a food processor or mouli, or mash coarsely with a fork.

Cheese & Potato Bake

This is one of the staples at my son's day nursery, where they have apparently never come across a child who doesn't love it. Among older children, it is even more popular when baked beans appear as an accompaniment. I generally use Cheddar cheese, but Gruyère or Gouda could be used as a change.

MAKES 8–10 PORTIONS

450 g/1 lb floury potatoes
a little butter and milk for mashing

150 g/5 oz tub cottage cheese
100 g/4 oz Cheddar cheese, grated

Boil the potatoes in unsalted water until tender. Drain and mash them to a smooth consistency with a little butter and milk. Stir in the cottage cheese and half the grated Cheddar. Pile the mixture into a shallow gratin dish and sprinkle the remaining Cheddar over the top. Place under a preheated grill until the cheese is melted and golden.

Ratatouille

My son used to adore ratatouille mixed with mashed potato and sprinkled with grated cheese. Pasta shapes or boiled rice are also good accompaniments.

MAKES 8–10 PORTIONS

salt
1 large aubergine, sliced
2 courgettes, sliced
30 ml/2 tablespoons olive oil
1 large onion, peeled and chopped

1 clove garlic, peeled and finely chopped
½ green pepper, seeded and chopped
½ red pepper, seeded and chopped
200 g/7 oz can chopped tomatoes
1 tablespoon chopped basil

Sprinkle salt on the aubergine and courgette slices, place them in a colander and cover with a heavy weight. Leave for 30 minutes to allow all the bitter juices to drain. Rinse thoroughly, dry on kitchen paper and chop.

Heat the oil, add the onion and fry gently until softened but not brown. Add the garlic, aubergine and courgettes and peppers, cover and cook gently for about 30 minutes, or until tender. Finally, add the tomatoes and basil and simmer, uncovered, for 30 minutes. For younger babies, purée the mixture before serving.

Bubble & Squeak

This seems to be one of the few ways of preparing cabbage that is acceptable to babies. When your child reaches the toddler stage, you can form the mixture into small patties and fry until crispy and golden to serve with vegetarian sausages or burgers. Let your child hear the mixture cooking as it really does live up to its name.

MAKES 8–10 PORTIONS

350 g/12 oz floury potatoes
350 g/12 oz spring greens
1 leek, washed and very finely chopped

50 ml/2 fl oz milk
knob of butter

Peel and dice the potatoes and boil for about 20 minutes, or until tender. Meanwhile, thoroughly wash the spring greens, discarding any dark, bitter leaves, and cutting out any tough pieces of stalk. Shred the leaves finely and steam for about 20 minutes, or until very tender. Poach the leek gently in the milk until soft, about 10 minutes. Mash the potatoes with the leek and milk mixture, add a little butter and stir in the spring greens.

Spinach, Potato & Leek Curry

Don't be perturbed by the idea of feeding your baby curry. This very delicately spiced dish has no chillies and is as far removed from a Friday night vindaloo as flock wallpaper is from frescoes. As a result of introducing Krishnan to a moderate amount of spice at an early age he has always been decidedly less intimidated by new flavours than many of his peers.

MAKES 12 PORTIONS

225 g/8 oz frozen leaf spinach
15 ml/1 tablespoon vegetable oil
50 g/2 oz leek, finely chopped
1 clove garlic, peeled and finely chopped
225 g/8 oz potatoes, peeled and cubed

1 medium tomato, skinned, seeded and finely chopped
15 ml/1 tablespoon natural yoghurt
¼ teaspoon garam masala

Cook the frozen spinach according to the directions on the packet. Drain, squeezing out as much water as you can, then chop finely in a food processor. Heat the oil, add the leek and garlic and fry until soft. Add the potatoes, spinach and tomato, fry for 2 minutes, then add the yoghurt and continue frying until you have a creamy consistency. Add a little water, cover and simmer until the potatoes are very tender. Sprinkle the garam masala on to the vegetable mixture, cook for a further 5 minutes, then mash or purée according to the age of your baby. Serve with either fingers of plain nan or pitta bread (most supermarkets sell acceptable versions), or rice, and a little plain yoghurt.

Lentil Sambhar

Most babies love the nutty sweetness of coconut, which in this dish combines beautifully with the fresh flavours of vegetables.

MAKES 12 PORTIONS

75 g/3 oz red lentils, washed and picked over
½ clove garlic, peeled and finely sliced
1 thin slice root ginger, peeled

100 g /4 oz mixed vegetables
(e.g. cauliflower, green beans, potatoes)
1 medium tomato, peeled, seeded and chopped
25 g/1 oz creamed coconut, grated

Place the lentils in a pan with the garlic and ginger, cover with water and simmer until very tender (about 30–40 minutes), adding extra water as required. Discard the ginger after this stage. Meanwhile, cut the vegetables into bite-sized pieces and steam until tender. Add the tomato and grated coconut to the cooked lentils, stir well and simmer for a further 5–10 minutes. Stir the prepared vegetables into the lentils. Mash or purée to the desired consistency. Serve with rice.

Vegetable Goulash

Paprika is a very good spice to introduce at an early age, as babies seem to appreciate its piquant sweetness. For older babies, you could try adding a few caraway seeds to give a more authentic flavour.

MAKES 12 PORTIONS

10 ml/2 teaspoons vegetable oil
½ small onion, peeled and finely diced
1 small carrot, peeled and finely chopped
½ green pepper, peeled, seeded
and finely chopped
½ red pepper, peeled, seeded
and finely chopped
pinch mild paprika

100 g/4 oz mushrooms, wiped and chopped
1 medium potato, peeled and diced
30 ml/2 tablespoons tomato purée
200 g/7 oz can red kidney beans, washed
and drained
100 g/4 oz basmati rice, cooked
15–30 ml/1–2 tablespoons natural yoghurt

Heat the oil, add the onion, carrot, peppers and paprika, and fry gently until softened but not browned. Add the mushrooms, cover and cook gently for 15 minutes. Add the potato, tomato purée and drained beans and allow to simmer for 30 minutes, or until the potato is very tender, adding a little extra water if required. Mix the rice into the cooked vegetables. Add the yoghurt. Mash or purée to the desired consistency.

Courgette Gratin

The creamy consistency of this delicately flavoured vegetable bake never fails to please young gourmands. My son used to like it with a purée of garden peas or broad beans and some crusty French bread to dip in and suck. Note that this recipe makes quite a large quantity and does not freeze well, so it is best for occasions when there are a few mouths to feed.

MAKES 10 PORTIONS

25 g/1 oz butter
25 g/1 oz plain flour
250 ml/8 fl oz milk
50 g/2 oz Emmental/Gruyère cheese, grated

pinch of grated nutmeg
225g/8 oz courgettes, wiped and chopped
40 g/1½ oz fresh white breadcrumbs

Melt the butter, stir in the flour and cook, stirring continuously, for 2 minutes. Gradually blend in the milk. Remove the sauce from the heat, stir in the cheese and nutmeg and allow to cool. Meanwhile, steam the courgettes for 5–10 minutes or until tender. Dry on kitchen paper and stir into the cheese sauce. Transfer the mixture to a shallow gratin dish, sprinkle the breadcrumbs over the top and bake at 400°F (200°C) Gas Mark 6 for 15–20 minutes, or until bubbling and brown.

SWEET TREATS

Fruity Fool

Custard made with commercial custard powder is fine for this recipe. (Choose a brand which is free from colouring and additives.) I have used strawberries, as they are Krishnan's favourite, but you could try raspberries (sieve the raspberry purée to remove the pips) or blueberries, adding a little sugar or concentrated apple juice if the fruit is too tart. Prunes canned in fruit juice are also excellent.

MAKES 6 PORTIONS

225 g/8 oz strawberries, washed and hulled
150 ml/5 fl oz thick custard

150 ml/5 fl oz Greek yoghurt

Purée the strawberries in a blender or food processor, then add the custard and yoghurt and blend for about 30 seconds. Pour into individual serving dishes (ramekins are a good size) and chill thoroughly before serving.

Rice Pudding

Traditional rice pudding couldn't be easier to make, and babies love it warm or cold. I find that the added evaporated milk in this recipe gives the pudding a delicious creamy richness. To vary the recipe, add a few washed raisins or sultanas, or chopped dried apricots.

MAKES 10 PORTIONS

600 ml/1 pint milk (use a small can of evaporated milk and make up the quantity with ordinary milk)

65 g/2½ oz pudding rice
25 g/1 oz sugar
a little grated nutmeg (optional)

Grease a shallow ovenproof dish and place the milk, rice and sugar in it. Sprinkle the nutmeg over the top, if using. Cover with foil and bake in a pre-heated oven at 300°F (150°C) Gas Mark 2 for 2 hours.

Banana Porridge

Serve this either for breakfast or as a pudding. This recipe will freeze if the banana is left out, then added just before serving.

MAKES 4–6 PORTIONS

300 ml/½ pint milk
40 g/1½ oz porridge oats

1 small banana

Pour the milk into a saucepan, sprinkle the porridge oats into the milk and bring to the boil, stirring all the time. Simmer for 1–2 minutes (or according to the instructions on the packet) until creamy, then remove from the heat. Allow to cool. Mash the banana and stir it into the oats until thoroughly combined.

Juicy Jelly

Jelly is an easy food for your baby to eat and a great accompaniment to yoghurt, cold custard or ice cream. Commercial jellies use gelatine as a setting agent, which is derived from the boiled-down bones and hooves of animal carcasses. One alternative is Vegegel, available from good supermarkets. This recipe uses agar agar (available from health food shops) and fruit juice to make a healthy alternative.

MAKES 8 PORTIONS

5 ml/1 teaspoon agar agar
300 ml/½ pint fruit juice (pear, apple and blackcurrant, or apple and strawberry are all good)

100 g/4 oz finely chopped fresh fruit, e.g. bananas, kiwi fruit, peeled peaches, strawberries (optional)

Dissolve the agar agar according to the instructions on the packet and stir into the juice. Add the chopped fruit, if using. Pour the jelly into one large mould or several individual ones, and chill until set.

Chocolate Pudding

Krishnan used to love this pudding with slices of ripe, peeled pear to dip into it.
Be warned, however – on the mess scale of 1–10, this dish rates 15!

MAKES 5 PORTIONS

*10 ml/2 teaspoons high-quality
cocoa powder*
5 ml/1 teaspoon raw cane sugar

15 ml/1 tablespoon cornflour
300 ml/½ pint milk

Dissolve the cocoa powder, sugar and cornflour in a little of the milk. Heat the remaining milk until almost boiling, pour it on to the cocoa paste and stir well. Return the mixture to the pan and bring to the boil, stirring continuously, until the mixture has thickened. Allow to cool. Chill before serving.

Baby Muesli

Commercial baby cereals are often overpriced, and contain excessive amounts of refined sugar. The coconut in this muesli provides the sweetness babies enjoy, without empty calories. I soak the muesli in breast milk or formula milk overnight to give it a creamy consistency. You could add grated apple and chopped banana (and ground nuts, for older children) before serving to make it even more nutritious.

MAKES 8–10 PORTIONS

50 g/2 oz oats
1 Weetabix biscuit

15 ml/1 tablespoon desiccated coconut

Place all the ingredients in a food processor and work to a fine powder. Store the prepared muesli in an airtight container.

SIX TO NINE MONTHS MENU CHART

Now that your baby is less reliant on milk feeds, aim to offer as wide a variety of foods as possible. This is easier because gluten and non-dairy products can now be tolerated.

INGREDIENTS CHECKLIST

Agar agar
Bread
Cheese
Chickpeas, canned
Cocoa powder
Coconut: creamed and desiccated
Cottage cheese
Couscous, pasta shapes and rice
Custard
Dried fruit
Eggs
Fresh fruit & vegetables
Fromage frais
Frozen spinach
Fruit juice
Herbs and spices
Oats
Passata
Pear and apple spread
Red lentils
Tahini
Tomatoes, canned
Weetabix
Yoghurt, Greek

* Repeat after lunch and before tea.

	Breakfast	Sleep*	Lunch	Tea	Bedtime
Day 1	Weetabix with banana	Breast or bottle milk	Cheese & Potato Bake Baked apple Juice	Parsnip & Apple Soup Melon Juice	Breast or bottle milk
Day 2	**Baby Muesli** with grated pear	Breast or bottle milk	Pasta with Napolitana Pasta Sauce Fromage frais Juice	Broccoli & Cauliflower Cheese Papaya Juice	Breast or bottle milk
Day 3	**Banana Porridge**	Breast or bottle milk	Khichri Chocolate Pudding Juice	Ten-minute Tomato Soup Toast soldiers Fromage frais Juice	Breast or bottle milk
Day 4	Mashed hard-boiled egg yolk Toast soldiers **Apricot Purée**	Breast or bottle milk	Fruity Couscous Fruity Fool Juice	Spinach, Potato & Leek Curry Juicy Jelly Juice	Breast or bottle milk
Day 5	Weetabix with chopped peaches	Breast or bottle milk	Pasta with Hummus Pasta Sauce Kiwi fruit Juice	Ratatouille Mashed potato Fromage frais Juice	Breast or bottle milk
Day 6	**Baby Muesli** with stewed prunes	Breast or bottle milk	Spring Vegetable Risotto Pear Juice	Sandwiches of Grated Cheese with Pear & Apple Spread Rice Pudding Juice	Breast or bottle milk
Day 7	Porridge with stewed plums	Breast or bottle milk	Lentil Sambhar Mashed banana Juice	Avocado & Cottage Cheese Dip Crudités Fromage frais	Breast or bottle milk

CHAPTER FOUR

The Independent Spirit
NINE TO TWELVE MONTHS

As your baby approaches his or her first birthday, rate of growth begins to slow down and curiosity and individuality accelerate. As far as feeding is concerned, appetite is no longer the sole contributory factor to mealtime success, if success is equated with introducing the maximum amount of nourishment in the minimum time with the minimum of fuss and mess. There is an old Hindu proverb which Krishnan's father tells me translates roughly as 'Your children teach you patience when no-one else can.' This is just as well, as, for the next few years you will need plenty of patience, particularly at mealtimes.

By now, your baby will almost certainly have graduated to a high chair and gained a few teeth and, in keeping with this newly elevated status, will no longer tolerate the ignominy of being forced to eat certain foods by a dominant adult. Having seen the pilot and worked out the screenplay, your baby now wants to be part of the action. Of course, clever parents will let baby think that they are just extras in the big production. The first step towards this is to include some finger foods at every meal (even just a few chunks of steamed vegetable) to give your baby a sense of autonomy.

Now is a good time to invest in suction-based bowls, spill-proof cups, extra feeding spoons (so that you can sneak in mouthfuls while your baby is pushing one piece of pasta round the bowl) and an industrial-sized box of washing powder. Make the feeding process less fraught by trying to allow time for your baby to play while eating. This may be easier said than done when you have to get out to work in 10 minutes and junior is still engrossed in making Weetabix mountains, but, as he or she is not going to compromise for some time, you may have to, perhaps by setting the alarm earlier!

The good news is that, for the most part, you will no longer need to prepare special meals (although you will still need to salt your own food separately), freeze food in ice-cube-sized portions or forgo interesting flavours. You should still moderate fat and sugar intake, peel raw fruit, and avoid whole nuts, honey, raw eggs and unpasteurised cheeses, but almost anything else goes. You should now find it possible to select something suitable for your baby to eat from most menus, even if it's only bread and cheese, although when travelling it's wise to take a few sandwiches, some fruit and a drink.

COMPROMISING SITUATIONS
As conscientious parents, it is all too easy to be seduced into the myth of an ideal eating pattern and try to enforce this upon our children while ignoring the fact that, like us, babies are individuals with rights to preferences, so long as they are not harmful. What really matters is to establish a routine that suits both you and your child. Some babies demand breakfast immediately on waking and prefer their morning milk before a sleep. My son liked milk on waking and breakfast an hour or so later, and attempts to reverse this pattern proved futile.

Likewise, you should not expect your baby to relish everything you introduce – some flavours are acquired tastes. If your baby rejects a particular dish, try reintroducing it at a later stage. If after several attempts this particular food is still a no-go zone, you can assume that it is actively disliked, and is not just being rejected for its unfamiliarity. It may also be that your baby is a 'grazer' rather than a 'stoker'; in which case, try to adapt your routine to allow smaller, more frequent meals.

Your own instincts should tell you when your baby is being wilful for the sake of it, and when he or she is acting out of genuine desire. Teething, for example, can make some babies very out of sorts and may upset eating patterns. Try offering chilled chunks of fruit to soothe inflamed gums in-between meals, and don't be concerned if your baby reverts to a more milk-based diet for a few days when teething.

BALANCING ACT

Older babies still require at least 600 ml/1 pint of milk per day. Not all of this need be taken as pure liquid milk – custards, white sauces and cooked dishes can all contribute to the quota. Most babies enjoy a substantial bottle or breast feed at bedtime and this is to be encouraged, for comfort and sustenance. In addition, offer as wide a variety of foods as possible, with plenty of soft, well-cooked fruit and vegetables, some dairy or vegetable protein (e.g. cheese or pulses) and cereals.

Most clinics will offer vitamin drops as dietary supplements, particularly during winter when keeping your baby well wrapped against the weather restricts exposure to daylight, which is vital for the production of vitamin D. By all means, accept these supplements as a precautionary measure, but never regard them as a substitute for a healthy diet.

If you feel that your baby could benefit from vitamin drops, it would be a good idea, if he or she is vegetarian, to opt for the ones which contain iron. As an alternative to vitamin drops, you could give your baby one of the brands of follow-on milk. These contain more of vitamins A, C and D, plus iron and a good balance of other vitamins and minerals. Follow-on milk is not necessary if you are still using formula milk, which is fine for babies up to twelve months.

SNACKS

At about this age, babies develop an interest in food outside mealtimes. Friends and relatives may well encourage this tendency by offering treats. There is nothing wrong with allowing your baby to eat outside of regular mealtimes, but do try to monitor the sorts of foods eaten at these times.

An occasional chocolate or biscuit will do no harm, but tastes developed in early childhood tend to stay into adult life, so it is better to encourage healthier nibbles from the very beginning. Breadsticks, cheese straws, well-washed dried fruit, and pieces of fresh fruit or vegetable are all good choices.

PREPARATION

Like most first-time mothers, I was positively evangelical about sterilising every piece of feeding equipment throughout the first year. While I still firmly believe that bottles used for milk should be sterilised for as long as your baby drinks from them (it is almost impossible to clean the inside of a teat thoroughly), I now realise what a complete waste of time this was, as, from the moment your baby is sitting up, every toy, object and bit of dirt within reach makes straight for the mouth.

Provided that you wash your baby's feeding equipment in hot soapy water and rinse it thoroughly, there is no need to take further precautions. To minimise the risk of stomach upsets, never save food that has been touched by the spoon your baby is using, and always throw away unfinished milk.

You will notice that most of the following recipes advocate steaming vegetables wherever possible. This is because steaming has been shown to preserve more of the vital nutrients than boiling, as well as being generally less detrimental to texture. Shallow-frying food, using a good-quality olive oil, is acceptable (see Falafel, Polenta, Cheese & Peanut Bites), but avoid deep-frying. You can introduce roast vegetables at this age (roast potatoes and parsnips are especially appreciated). When roasting, brush the vegetables lightly with oil, (don't sit them in a pool of it) and blot them well with kitchen paper before serving.

Where fresh rather than canned pulses are stipulated (this is relatively rare because I personally believe that life is too short for soaking lentils), always boil them rapidly for at least 10 minutes to destroy potentially harmful toxins. When substituting dried pulses for canned, use half the stated quantity, as they will roughly double in weight when soaked.

For freezing foods, it's worth buying two or three trays of stacking plastic pots as, while it may be ecologically sound to use discarded yoghurt cartons to freeze baby-sized portions, I found these difficult to seal and label, and prone to splitting.

TEXTURE

Many of the following recipes may be fed to babies without additional processing. As emphasised in the previous chapter, it is important to introduce texture if you don't wish to end up with a picky toddler who balks at anything bulkier than a chocolate button. Babies are creatures of habit, so if they are fed mush, then mush is all they will want (though some babies progress more quickly than others to lumpy food, and it may depend on whether they are early or late teethers). Make the change gradual. At the beginning of this phase, process food for just a few seconds, introduce grated food alongside purées and try to contrast textures. Should you be firmly convinced that your baby is congenitally incapable of coping with lumps, offer a chocolate finger biscuit and see what happens!

SOUPS, SALADS AND SAVOURIES

Apollo Soup

This homely, Italian-style soup is a meal in itself. My son loved it with garlic bread. Once he was old enough to enjoy it unprocessed he insisted that we make it using spaceship noodles – hence the very un-Italian title.

MAKES 12 PORTIONS

15 ml/1 tablespoon olive oil
1 small onion, peeled
and chopped
1 clove garlic, peeled
and finely chopped
6 large ripe tomatoes,
peeled, seeded
and chopped

350 g/12 oz canned cannellini beans,
washed and drained
200 g/7 oz tiny pasta shapes
1 tablespoon chopped flat-leaf parsley
50 g/2 oz cheese, grated
1 litre/1½ pints vegetable stock
black pepper to taste
a little chopped fresh basil (optional)

Heat the oil and gently fry the onion until soft. Add the garlic, tomatoes, beans, pasta, parsley, two-thirds of the cheese, and the stock. Season with a little black pepper, if liked, then bring to the boil and simmer for about 30 minutes. Stir in the basil, if using, allow to cool slightly and purée coarsely in a food processor. To serve, sprinkle with the remaining cheese.

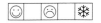

Pumpkin & Apple Soup

I devised this soup on Krishnan's first Hallowe'en as a way of using up the surfeit of pumpkin flesh left from my clumsy attempts at making Hallowe'en lanterns. Try serving it with apple crisps (from health food shops and some supermarkets) for your baby to dunk.

MAKES 6 PORTIONS

knob of butter
5 ml/1 teaspoon vegetable oil
100 g/4 oz onion, peeled and chopped
225 g/8 oz pumpkin flesh, finely diced

225 g/8 oz apples, peeled, cored and chopped
300 ml/½ pint vegetable stock
300 ml/½ pint apple juice

Heat the butter and oil together in a large saucepan, add the onion and fry for 5–10 minutes, or until softened but not brown. Add the pumpkin flesh and apples, stir well, cover, and sweat over a low heat for 20 minutes, stirring occasionally. Pour in the vegetable stock and apple juice, bring to the boil and simmer for 30 minutes or until the vegetables are meltingly tender. Allow to cool slightly, and blend to a smooth consistency.

☺	☹	❄

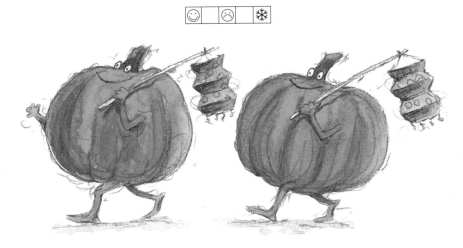

Sesame Breadsticks

Breadsticks are much healthier for babies to munch on than biscuits and they are ideal to appease a ravenous infant to whom the phrase 'ready in five minutes' means nothing. Because they harden as they cool, they're also very soothing for teething babies. They are easy to make, if a little time-consuming, and they store well in an airtight container.

MAKES ABOUT 32

7 g sachet fast-action dried yeast
450 g/1 lb strong white flour
50 g/2 oz butter
60 ml/4 tablespoons olive oil

200 ml/7 fl oz tepid water
1 free-range egg, beaten
4 level tablespoons sesame seeds

Place the yeast and flour in a large bowl and make a well in the centre. Place the butter and oil in a small saucepan and heat until all the butter has melted. Add the tepid water to the butter and oil mixture and pour this into the well in the flour. Mix to a dough, then turn out on to a floured surface and knead for 10 minutes, or until the dough is smooth and elastic.

Divide the dough into 32 pieces and, using the floured palms of your hands, roll into sausage shapes about 20 cm/8 in long. Arrange the sticks on greased baking sheets (leaving room for the mixture to swell). Brush with beaten egg, sprinkle with sesame seeds and bake in an oven preheated to 400°F (200°C) Gas Mark 6 for about 20 minutes, or until golden. Turn off the heat and allow the breadsticks to cool and become crisp in the oven.

Cheese Straws

Cheese straws provide another tasty and nutritious nibble. For a more substantial snack, serve these with any of the dips in the preceding and following pages.

MAKES ABOUT 40

100 g/4 oz wholemeal flour
25 g/1 oz mixed nuts,
finely chopped, or ground

50 g/2 oz butter
50 g/2 oz Cheddar cheese, grated
1 free-range egg, beaten

Sift the flour and stir in the nuts. Rub the butter into the flour. Stir in the cheese, add the egg and work to a dough. Knead lightly. Roll out on a lightly floured board to approximately 6 mm/¼ in. Cut into thin fingers. Bake on oiled baking sheets in an oven preheated to 375°F (190°C) Gas Mark 5 for 12–15 minutes.

Maple Syrup-glazed Corn

Corn is universally loved by babies and children. This method of cooking gives a lovely sweet result, and your baby will enjoy gnawing at the juicy kernels.

MAKES 3–4 PORTIONS

1 corn on the cob
15 g/½ oz butter

5 ml/1 teaspoon pure maple syrup
a little chopped parsley

Cut the corn crossways into 3 or 4 slices (they should be of a size that your baby can grasp) and cook in boiling water for 5–10 minutes, or until the kernels are tender. Drain and dry. Melt the butter and maple syrup together in a small frying pan and add the corn. Cook gently for about 5 minutes, turning frequently and ensuring that the maple syrup does not burn. Sprinkle the parsley over the corn and serve.

Cheese & Peanut Bites

Babies love these tasty savouries with tomato or apple purée as a dip. They also make a great portable snack.

MAKES ABOUT 12

185 g/6 oz fresh white
breadcrumbs
100 g/4 oz grated Cheddar cheese
1 small onion, chopped

1 small carrot, chopped
1 tablespoon chopped parsley
15 ml/1 tablespoon smooth peanut butter
2 free-range eggs, separated

Place two-thirds of the breadcrumbs in the bowl of a food processor with the cheese, onion, carrot and parsley and process until fine. Add the peanut butter and egg yolks and process again until the mixture holds together. Divide the mixture into 12 pieces and roll them into balls. Dip each ball in egg white, then coat them in the remaining breadcrumbs. Place the coated balls on an oiled baking sheet and bake in an oven preheated to 375°F (190°C) Gas Mark 5 for about 20 minutes (turning them after 10 minutes) until crisp and golden. Serve warm or cold.

Minty Yoghurt Dip

As well as being good with Falafel, this mild, refreshing dip is delicious with sticks of raw carrot or cucumber. Krishnan used to adore it with fingers of warm nan bread.

MAKES 5 PORTIONS

2.5 cm/1 in piece cucumber
150 ml/5 fl oz Greek yoghurt
1 teaspoon finely chopped mint

Peel, grate and drain the cucumber. Combine the Greek yoghurt, cucumber and finely chopped mint and leave for at least 30 minutes to allow the flavours to develop fully.

☺ | ☹ |

Falafel

These mildly spicy Middle Eastern savouries make an excellent finger food for babies. If you are apprehensive about giving your baby exotic flavours you could omit the spices altogether – the falafel will still taste good.

MAKES 12

400 g/14 oz can chickpeas, rinsed
and drained
1 small onion, finely chopped
1 small red pepper, seeded, finely chopped
and steamed until tender
1 clove garlic, peeled and finely chopped

1 tablespoon chopped flat-leaf parsley
¼ teaspoon ground cumin
¼ teaspoon ground coriander
1 free-range egg, beaten
a little flour for coating
15 ml/1 tablespoon vegetable oil

Place the first seven ingredients in the bowl of a food processor and work to a coarse purée. Add the egg and blend again briefly to combine. Divide the mixture into 12 and, using the palms of your hands, shape into little 'sausages'. Roll each lightly in flour and chill for 30 minutes.

Heat the oil in a frying pan and cook the falafel gently over a medium heat for about 10 minutes, turning frequently, until golden. Serve with tomato purée or Minty Yoghurt Dip.

☺ | ☹ |

Apple, Beetroot & Carrot Salad

It's a good idea to introduce your baby to salads as soon as larger quantities of raw vegetables are acceptable, otherwise unfamiliarity will breed contempt. Just as adults aren't enthralled by a lettuce leaf and a slice of cucumber, babies too like colourful interesting combinations.

MAKES 4 PORTIONS

1 carrot, washed, peeled and finely grated
50 g/2 oz cooked beetroot, finely grated
½ apple, peeled, cored and finely chopped
1 tablespoon raisins, washed

7 ml/½ tablespoon olive oil
½ teaspoon cider vinegar
pinch of sugar

Place the carrot, beetroot, apple and raisins in a bowl and stir well to combine. Mix together the olive oil and cider vinegar and season with a little sugar. Pour this dressing over the vegetables and fruit and toss to combine. Serve with grated cheese.

Muffin Pizzas

While your baby is still consuming diminutive portions, it seems hardly worth making fresh pizza dough in tiny quantities. For a speedy teatime treat, bought muffins make an acceptable pizza base and this simple topping couldn't be easier to prepare.

MAKES 4 PORTIONS

2 muffins
200 g/7 oz can chopped tomatoes
15 ml/1 tablespoon olive oil

75 g/3 oz grated mozzarella cheese
1 teaspoon chopped oregano

S plit the muffins. Place the tomatoes in a small frying pan, add the oil, bring to the boil and simmer for 15 minutes, stirring occasionally, until thickened. Drain off any excess liquid, sieve the tomato sauce to remove the seeds, then purée and allow to cool. Spoon equal amounts of the tomato sauce on to the muffin halves, place the cheese on the tomato, then sprinkle the oregano on top. Bake in an oven preheated to 450°F (230°C) Gas Mark 8 for 10 –12 minutes, or until the pizzas are golden brown and bubbling.

☺ ☹

Rice Salad

Don't be tempted to use leftover rice for this appealing salad, unless the rice is still warm – heat is needed to develop the flavours. Pepper, corn and peas are always popular with babies but you could also try green beans, mushrooms or broad beans. For added sweetness, a little fresh pineapple or orange also work well.

MAKES 10 PORTIONS

150 g/5 oz basmati rice
½ small red pepper, seeded, finely chopped
and steamed until tender
50 g/2 oz frozen peas, cooked
50 g/2 oz frozen sweetcorn, cooked

25 g/1 oz currants
30 ml/2 tablespoons olive oil
15 ml/1 tablespoon orange juice
½ clove garlic, crushed
a little chopped flat-leaf parsley

C ook the rice until tender, stir well using a fork and allow to cool slightly. Add the cooked vegetables and currants and stir well. Mix together the oil, orange juice and garlic, pour this dressing over the rice mixture and stir well to combine. Allow to cool completely. Before serving, sprinkle the parsley over the salad and stir again.

☺ ☹

Avocado & Orange Salad

Avocados are a valuable source of vitamins and most babies seem to enjoy their creamy texture. Choose a very sweet variety of orange or, to ring the changes, substitute a sweet dessert pear for the orange.

MAKES 4 PORTIONS

1 *very ripe avocado*
1 *orange*

Peel and stone the avocado and cut it into small chunks. Using a sharp knife, cut off the top and base of the orange and then peel away the skin. Carefully make incisions between the pith and the orange so that you are left with skinless segments. Reserve any juice. Chop the orange segments in half and combine with the avocado. Add the orange juice and toss again. Serve at once with fingers of brown bread.

PASTA SAUCES

Busy mothers will probably identify with my belief that you can never have too many pasta sauces in your repertoire. The four that follow are all good with any pasta shapes. Now that your baby is older, try offering him some of the many excellent stuffed pastas available – Krishnan especially liked mushroom and cheese, and spinach and ricotta.

Spinach & Ricotta Pasta Sauce

MAKES 8 PORTIONS

25 g/1 oz butter
225 g/8 oz frozen chopped leaf
spinach, thawed

a little grated nutmeg
100 g/4 oz ricotta cheese
25 g/1 oz pecorino cheese, grated

Melt the butter and, when it is bubbling, add the spinach. Fry gently until the spinach is heated through. Season with the grated nutmeg. Stir in the ricotta and pecorino cheeses and heat gently without boiling. Serve with pasta shapes.

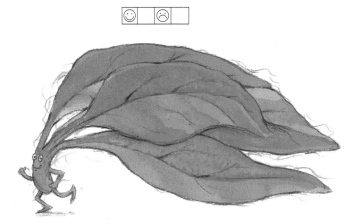

Three-pepper Pasta Sauce

MAKES 6 PORTIONS

30 ml/2 tablespoons olive oil
1 clove garlic, finely chopped
1 medium red pepper, seeded and
finely sliced
1 medium green pepper, seeded and
finely sliced

1 medium yellow pepper, seeded and
finely sliced
1 onion, peeled and thinly sliced
½ teaspoon dried oregano
a little chopped fresh basil
2 large tomatoes, peeled, seeded
and chopped

Heat the oil, add the garlic, peppers, onion and herbs. Cover and cook over a very low heat for about 20 minutes, or until the vegetables are very tender. Add the chopped tomatoes, raise the heat and allow the mixture to bubble. Remove from the heat and purée in a food processor.

Broccoli Pasta Sauce

MAKES 4 PORTIONS

225 g/8 oz broccoli florets
25 g/1 oz butter
20 g/¾ oz plain flour
300 ml/½ pint milk

1 bay leaf
1 slice onion
2 sprigs parsley (stalks left on)
a little grated nutmeg

Cut the broccoli florets into bite-sized pieces and steam for about 5 minutes, until tender but not wilted. Set aside. Melt the butter, stir in the flour and add the milk, whisking until the sauce bubbles and is thickened and smooth. Drop the bay leaf, onion and parsley into the sauce, lower the heat and simmer for 15–20 minutes, stirring occasionally and adding extra milk if the sauce thickens too much. Remove the onion, bay leaf and parsley, season the sauce with a little grated nutmeg and stir in the cooked broccoli.

Mushroom & Four-cheese Pasta Sauce

MAKES 4 PORTIONS

15 g/½ oz butter
½ onion, peeled and finely chopped
1 clove garlic, finely chopped
100 g/4 oz button mushrooms, wiped and quartered

25 g/1 oz each Bel Paese, Cheddar, Gruyère and pecorino cheese, grated
150 ml/5 fl oz single cream

Melt the butter and gently fry the onion and garlic until softened but not browned. Add the mushrooms and fry for a further 5 minutes. Remove from the heat, add the cheeses and cream, and stir until melted (you may need to return the pan to the heat to achieve this but do not let the sauce boil).

MAIN COURSES

Lentil Hot Pot

In our house this dish is irreverently known as 'bottom of the fridge stew', because it invariably appears when I have put off going shopping and am left with a few store-cupboard standbys. Despite the frugal ingredients, it tastes quite sumptuous.

MAKES 10 PORTIONS

15 ml/1 tablespoon vegetable oil
1 onion, peeled and chopped
1 clove garlic, crushed
1 large potato, peeled and cubed
2 carrots, peeled and diced
2 celery sticks, washed and chopped

225 g/8 oz red lentils, washed and picked over
400 g/14 oz can chopped tomatoes
10 ml/2 teaspoons tomato purée
1 bay leaf
½ teaspoon dried oregano
600 ml/1 pint vegetable stock

Heat the oil and fry the onion and garlic until softened but not browned. Add the potatoes, carrots, celery and lentils, and stir to coat the vegetables with the oil. Now add the tomatoes, tomato purée, herbs and the vegetable stock. Bring to the boil, cover and simmer for 40–45 minutes, or until the lentils and vegetables are very tender. Remove the bay leaf. Mash the lentils and vegetables using a fork before serving.

Vegetable Crumble

Babies seem to love both sweet and savoury crumbles. This simple recipe lends itself to all sorts of vegetable permutations. Here I have used root vegetables and squash, but courgettes, cauliflower and peppers make a tasty and colourful alternative.

MAKES 10 PORTIONS

15 ml/1 tablespoon vegetable oil
1 onion, peeled and chopped
1 clove garlic, peeled and finely chopped
225 g/8 oz parsnip, peeled and cubed
225 g/8 oz swede, peeled and cubed
225 g/8 oz butternut squash, peeled and cubed
25 g/1 oz butter
25 g/1 oz plain flour
350 ml/12 fl oz milk

50 g/2 oz red Leicester cheese, grated
pinch of grated nutmeg
TOPPING
40 g/1½ oz softened butter
50 g/2 oz wholemeal flour
50 g/2 oz rolled oats
1 tablespoon chopped parsley and
chives (optional)
25 g/1 oz walnuts, toasted and ground

Heat the oil and gently fry the onion and garlic until softened but not browned. Meanwhile, steam the prepared vegetables for about 10 minutes or until tender. Stand the vegetables in a colander for a few minutes to allow any excess liquid to evaporate.

Melt the butter in a saucepan, add the flour and cook, stirring, for 2 minutes. Gradually incorporate the milk to form a smooth sauce, and simmer gently for 2 minutes. Remove the sauce from the heat and stir in the cheese and nutmeg. Add the cooked onions and vegetables to the sauce, mix thoroughly and transfer to an oiled gratin dish.

To make the crumble topping, rub the softened butter into the flour and oats, and stir in the herbs (if using) and nuts. Spoon the crumble over the vegetables and smooth the top. Bake in an oven preheated to 400°F (200°C) Gas Mark 6 for about 35 minutes, or until the topping is golden and the filling bubbling. Mash coarsely with a fork and serve with lightly steamed green beans or broccoli.

Vegetarian Shepherd's Pie

The texture of bulghar wheat is ideal for a shepherd's pie and adds extra nutrition to this tasty vegetarian version of a nursery favourite.

MAKES 6–8 PORTIONS

50 g/2 oz bulghar wheat
450 g/1 lb potatoes, peeled and cubed
a little butter and milk, for mashing
30 ml/2 tablespoons vegetable oil
1 onion, finely chopped
1 clove garlic, finely chopped
175 g/6 oz button mushrooms, wiped
and quartered

2 medium courgettes, wiped,
trimmed and diced
1 carrot, peeled and diced
2 tablespoons chopped fresh parsley
200 g/7 oz can chopped tomatoes
30 ml/2 tablespoons tomato purée
175 ml/6 fl oz vegetable stock
100 g/4 oz Cheddar cheese, grated

Place the bulghar wheat in a bowl, cover with boiling water and leave to stand for 15 minutes, or until the grain has absorbed the liquid. Stir well with a fork to fluff up. Boil the potatoes for about 15 minutes or until tender, drain and mash with a little butter and milk.

Heat the oil, add the onion and garlic and fry until softened but not browned. Add the mushrooms, courgettes and carrot and continue frying for 2 minutes. Stir in the parsley, tomatoes, tomato purée and stock. Bring to the boil, cover and simmer until the vegetables are tender, about 15 minutes.

Add the soaked bulghar wheat to the vegetables, stir and continue cooking for 5 minutes. Transfer the mixture to a shallow ovenproof dish and spread the mashed potato evenly on top, roughening the surface with a fork. Sprinkle the cheese over the top and bake in an oven preheated to 400°F (200°C) Gas Mark 6 for 30 minutes, or until golden. Serve with vegetarian gravy.

Barley Pot

When I was a child, barley broth was a regular wintertime supper and I remember loving the creamy texture of the shiny pearl-like grains of barley. Although it has been usurped by designer pastas as an ingredient in soups and stews, I think barley is still worth using. Krishnan used to love this barley pot served with garlic bread.

MAKES 3 PORTIONS

10 ml/2 teaspoons vegetable oil
½ clove of garlic, finely chopped
½ onion, peeled and chopped
1 small carrot, peeled and diced
2 celery sticks, washed and finely sliced
1 teaspoon mild paprika
300 ml/½ pint vegetable stock

200 g/7 oz can chopped tomatoes
20 g/¾ oz pearl barley, washed
1 leek, washed, trimmed and finely sliced
1 parsnip, peeled and cubed
175 g/6 oz cauliflower florets
½ teaspoon chopped rosemary (optional)

Heat the oil and fry the garlic, onion, carrot and celery for 5 minutes. Stir in the paprika and continue frying for a further minute. Add the remaining ingredients and simmer gently for about 40 minutes, or until the vegetables are tender. Mash coarsely before serving.

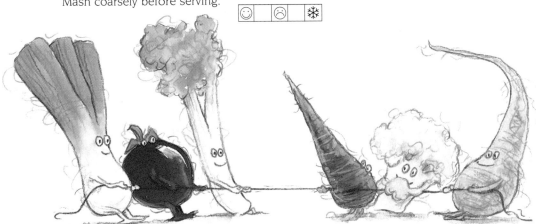

Potato Hash

This is a slightly more grown-up version of Krishnan's beloved Cheese & Potato Bake (see page 52). Petit pois and sweetcorn make good accompaniments.

MAKES 4 PORTIONS

350 g/12 oz new potatoes
15 g/½ oz butter
½ onion, peeled and finely chopped
1 beef tomato, peeled, seeded and chopped

85 ml/3 fl oz single cream
50 g/2 oz Cheddar cheese, grated
2–3 tablespoons wholemeal breadcrumbs

Scrub the potatoes and boil them in their skins. When they are tender, drain, cube and spread them over the base of a small, shallow gratin dish. Melt the butter over a very low heat and gently fry the onion until softened but not browned, then add the tomato and continue cooking for 5 minutes, or until the tomato is tender. Now add the cream and cheese to the onion and tomato, and stir continuously until the cheese is almost melted. Pour the sauce over the potatoes, sprinkle the breadcrumbs on top, and brown under a preheated grill.

☺ ☹

Lentil Moussaka

It Is one of the many small milestones of babyhood when you can actually look forward to sharing food with your baby. This was one of the first dishes that Krishnan and I enjoyed together. Puy lentils are small black lentils which have a superior flavour and texture to other varieties, but other lentils could be substituted.

MAKES ENOUGH FOR MUM, DAD AND BABY, OR 6 PORTIONS

225 g/8 oz puy lentils
1 large aubergine, wiped and trimmed
15 ml/1 tablespoon olive oil, plus a little
extra for brushing
1 small onion, peeled and finely sliced
1 small red pepper, seeded and thinly sliced
1 clove garlic, crushed

1 teaspoon dried mixed herbs
50 g/2 oz sun-dried tomatoes, drained of oil
and finely chopped
350 ml/12 fl oz passata
50 g/2 oz Cheddar cheese, grated
25 g/1 oz wholemeal breadcrumbs

Wash the lentils thoroughly. Place them in a saucepan, cover with cold water and bring to the boil. Boil rapidly for 10 minutes, then reduce the heat and simmer for 30–40 minutes, or until tender, then drain.

Slice the aubergine into rounds and place on a grill pan. Brush lightly with olive oil, grill until golden, then turn over and repeat the process. Set the cooked aubergine aside.

Heat the oil and gently fry the onion and pepper until soft. Stir in the garlic and turn off the heat. Place half the lentils in the base of an ovenproof dish, top with half the aubergines, half the onion and pepper mixture and half of both the sun-dried tomatoes and passata. Repeat the layers. Mix together the cheese and breadcrumbs and sprinkle them over the top. Bake in an oven preheated to 350°F (180°C) Gas Mark 4, for about 30 minutes, or until golden and bubbling. Purée coarsely before serving.

☺	☹

Hungarian Stuffed Marrow

I have always found marrow a bland and uninteresting vegetable, but Krishnan loves it – and, prepared in this way, it is both tasty and nutritious.

MAKES 4 PORTIONS

½ large marrow, cut lengthways
75 g/3 oz carrots, peeled and sliced
75 g/3 oz parsnips, peeled and chopped
approximately 85 ml/3 fl oz vegetable stock
15 g/½ oz butter
1 small onion, chopped
½ red pepper, seeded and diced

50 g/2 oz button mushrooms, wiped and quartered
200 g/7 oz can chopped tomatoes
50 g/2 oz frozen sweetcorn, defrosted
150 ml/5 fl oz Greek yoghurt
2 tablespoons mild paprika

Peel the marrow and remove the seeds and pith, leaving the flesh intact. Boil the marrow, still intact, for about 10 minutes, until softened (you will need a fish kettle or a large, deep stock pan). Drain the marrow, reserving the liquid. Boil the carrots and parsnips in this liquid until tender. Drain the carrots and parsnips (again reserving the liquid) and mash them together. Make up the reserved liquid to 150 ml/5 fl oz with vegetable stock, and set aside.

Melt the butter and gently fry the onion until softened but not browned. Add the pepper and continue frying for 10 minutes. Add the mashed carrot and parsnip to the pepper mixture, together with the mushrooms, and cook for a further 2 minutes. Stir in the tomatoes, sweetcorn and stock mixture. Bring to the boil and simmer for 25 minutes.

Mix together the yoghurt and paprika, add this to the vegetable mixture and stir well to combine. Pile this mixture into the shell of cooked marrow flesh, wrap in foil and bake in an oven preheated to 350°F (180°C) Gas Mark 4 for 45 minutes, or until the marrow is very tender. Cut the stuffed marrow into quarters and mash. Serve with rice and yoghurt.

Butterbean & Leek Gratin

Next to the perennially popular baked beans, butterbeans are my son's favourite pulse. They seem to have a natural affinity with the sweet pungency of leeks, which makes this dish a great success.

MAKES 10–12 PORTIONS

3 medium leeks, trimmed, washed and finely chopped
½ small cauliflower, divided into florets
25 g/1 oz butter
1 small onion, finely chopped
1 clove garlic, finely chopped
25 g/1 oz plain flour
1 teaspoon ground coriander

250 ml/8 fl oz mixed vegetable stock and milk
400 g/14 oz can butterbeans, rinsed and drained
50 g/2 oz Cheddar cheese, grated
1 small packet unsalted plain crisps, crushed

Steam the leeks and cauliflower for about 10 minutes, or until tender, and set aside. Melt the butter and gently fry the onion and garlic until softened but not browned. Sprinkle the flour on to the onion and continue cooking, stirring, for 3 minutes. Add the coriander, then stir in the stock and milk to form a smooth sauce (you may need to add a little more liquid to achieve a smooth consistency). Simmer the sauce gently for a couple of minutes.

Stir the beans, leeks and cauliflower into the sauce and transfer to an ovenproof dish. Mix together the cheese and crisps, and sprinkle them over the top of the vegetables. Bake in an oven preheated to 350°F (180°C) Gas Mark 4 for 30 minutes, until golden and bubbling. Mash with a fork or purée coarsely. Serve with steamed green vegetables.

Courgette, Cauliflower &
Chickpea Curry

This mild and creamy recipe contains the merest hint of spice and no chilli, so it is perfectly safe to give to your baby.

MAKES 12–15 PORTIONS

15 ml/1 tablespoon vegetable oil
1 small onion, finely chopped
25 g/1 oz plain flour
5–10 ml/1–2 teaspoons mild curry paste
15 ml/1 tablespoon tomato purée
2 tablespoons smooth peanut butter

600 ml/1 pint vegetable stock
½ medium cauliflower, divided into florets
4 medium courgettes, cubed
400 g/14 oz can chickpeas
300 ml/½ pint natural yoghurt

Heat the oil and fry the onion until softened but not browned. Sprinkle the flour over the onion and cook, stirring, for 2–3 minutes. Add the curry paste, tomato purée and peanut butter, and gradually stir in the stock. Simmer for 5–10 minutes.

Meanwhile, steam the cauliflower and courgettes until tender, about 5–12 minutes (add the courgettes after the cauliflower as they will take less time). Add the cauliflower, courgettes and chickpeas to the sauce, cover and simmer gently for 20–30 minutes. Turn off the heat and allow the curry to stand for 10 minutes before stirring in the yoghurt. Mash or purée and serve with rice and banana slices.

Chinese Fried Rice

If your baby enjoys pronounced flavours, you could add a little grated ginger and garlic to this dish (fried with the onion and carrot). Do make sure that the egg is thoroughly cooked before adding the rice. You could also add a few toasted sesame seeds before serving. Soy sauce is high in sodium, so it should be used with caution – this recipe contains just a dash.

MAKES 8 PORTIONS

15 ml/1 tablespoon vegetable oil
3 spring onions, trimmed and sliced
1 medium carrot, peeled and diced
½ green pepper, seeded and diced
50 g/2 oz frozen peas, defrosted
40 g/1½ oz beansprouts, washed

1 large tomato, peeled, seeded and chopped
1 free-range egg, beaten
225 g/8 oz cooked basmati rice
5 ml/1 teaspoon sesame oil
dash of soy sauce

Heat the oil in a large frying pan or wok, add the spring onions and carrot and stir-fry for a couple of minutes. Add the pepper, peas, beansprouts and tomato and stir-fry for a further 2 minutes. Push the vegetables to one side of the pan, pour in the beaten egg and cook, stirring continuously, until it is well scrambled. Add the rice, mix well, and stir-fry until it is heated through. Drizzle the sesame oil and soy sauce over the rice, and serve.

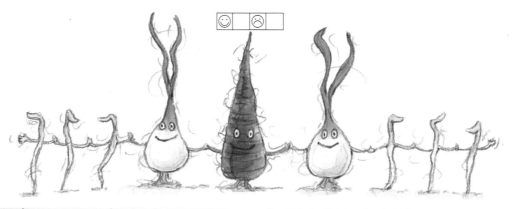

Polenta with Tomato Sauce

Polenta is a northern Italian staple made from cornmeal. Because it has rather a bland flavour and soft texture, it is ideal for babies. Serve it with the sweet tomato sauce recipe given below, or any of the pasta sauce recipes.

MAKES 8 PORTIONS

1 litre/1½ pints water
225 g/8 oz polenta
50 g/2 oz butter
SAUCE
15 ml/1 tablespoon olive oil
1 onion, finely chopped

1 clove garlic, finely chopped
2 red peppers, seeded and finely chopped
400 g/14 oz can of tomatoes
15 ml/1 tablespoon tomato purée
1 free-range egg, beaten
extra cornmeal for coating

Bring the water to the boil, gradually sprinkle the polenta on to the water and stir well until smooth. Add the butter, cover and cook for about 20 minutes, stirring frequently until thick and creamy. Pour the cooked polenta into an oiled dish about 33 cm x 23 cm (13 in x 9 in) and leave to cool and set.

To make the sauce, heat the oil and fry the onion and garlic until softened but not browned. Add the peppers and continue frying for 5 minutes. Now add the tomatoes and tomato purée, bring to the boil, cover and simmer for 20 minutes, or until the sauce is reduced. Cut the cold polenta into squares, coat with beaten egg and cornmeal and shallow-fry until golden brown. To serve, pour the sauce over the polenta.

SWEETS AND PUDDINGS

Apple & Raisin Muffins

These delectable, low-fat cakes are perfect for breakfast or tea, and can even be served with custard or ice cream for a more substantial pudding.

MAKES 12

300 ml/½ pint milk
100 g/4 oz oat bran
2 free-range eggs
65 g/2½ oz butter, melted
40 g/1½ oz raw cane sugar
½ teaspoon vanilla extract

50 g/2 oz wholemeal flour
100 g/4 oz plain flour
2 teaspoons baking powder
1 eating apple, peeled, cored and chopped
4 tablespoons raisins, soaked in orange juice
for a few hours

Grease 12 deep patty tins. Place the milk and oat bran in a bowl. Beat together the eggs, melted butter, sugar and vanilla extract. Add the egg mixture to the oat and milk mixture.

Sift the flours and baking powder together and stir in the chopped apple. Combine the two mixtures, add the soaked, drained raisins and stir thoroughly. Spoon the mixture into the prepared patty tins and bake in an oven preheated to 375°F (190°C) Gas Mark 5 for 25–30 minutes, or until golden and risen.

Oat Cookies

Oats are a valuable source of vitamins and fibre, so these wholesome, sugar-free biscuits are an ideal, enjoyable treat.

MAKES 24

100 g/4 oz wholemeal flour
100 g/4 oz rolled oats
100 g/4 oz butter, softened

4 tablespoons pear and apple spread
1 free-range egg, beaten

Place the flour and oats in a bowl and rub in the butter. Mix in the pear and apple spread (you may need to soften this first by warming it over a pan of hot water or in a microwave oven). Add the egg, and mix to a firm dough.

Roll out the dough on a lightly floured surface to about 6 mm/¼ in thick then stamp out into shapes using biscuit cutters. Place on greased baking sheets and bake in an oven preheated to 375°F (190°C) Gas Mark 5 for 10–15 minutes, or until golden. Allow to cool slightly on the trays before transferring to a wire rack to cool completely. Store in an airtight container.

Strawberry Crunch

My son very appropriately once described this as 'upside-down crumble'. If you don't want to use cream, thick custard is every bit as good.

MAKES 8 PORTIONS

75 g/3 oz butter
50 g/2 oz desiccated coconut
75 g/3 oz rolled oats
50 g/2 oz wholemeal flour

300 ml/½ pint whipped cream
150 ml/5 fl oz Greek yoghurt
225 g/8 oz strawberries, washed and hulled
a little toasted coconut to decorate

Place the butter, coconut, oats and flour in a food processor and work until the butter is well rubbed in. Grease a shallow baking tray and press the mixture in to a depth of 2.5 cm/1 in. Bake in an oven preheated to 375°F (190°C) Gas Mark 5 for about 20 minutes, or until golden. Leave the crunch to cool, cut it into sections and then crumble these to cover the base of a shallow serving dish. Whisk together the cream and yoghurt and spread this over the crunch base. Top with chopped strawberries and chill for at least one hour so that the base softens. To serve, decorate with toasted coconut.

Carrot Cake

Older babies enjoy cake as an occasional teatime treat, but plain sponges can be a little dry for them to cope with. Carrots make this cake very moist and therefore easy for babies to eat.

MAKES 12 PORTIONS

175 g/6 oz raw cane sugar
175 ml/6 fl oz sunflower oil
3 free-range eggs, beaten
225 g/8 oz carrots, peeled
and finely grated

grated rind of 1 orange
175 g/6 oz self-raising flour
½ teaspoon baking powder
1 teaspoon ground cinnamon
½ teaspoon grated nutmeg

In a mixing bowl or food processor, beat together the sugar, oil and eggs until well blended. Mix in the grated carrots and orange rind. Sift in the flour, baking powder and spices and mix thoroughly. Pour the mixture into a greased and lined 20 cm/8 in square cake tin and bake in a preheated oven at 350°F (180°C) Gas Mark 4 for 45 minutes, until well risen and a skewer inserted into the centre comes out clean. Cool on a wire rack, then store in an airtight container.

Blueberry & Peach Cobbler

Blueberries and peaches make quite the most delectable combination imaginable, second only to Krishnan's favourite, blueberry and strawberry.

MAKES 8 PORTIONS

450 g/1 lb ripe peaches
2 tablespoons caster sugar
pinch of grated nutmeg
pinch of grated cinnamon
½ teaspoon lemon juice
225 g/8 oz blueberries, washed and dried

TOPPING
50 g/2 oz plain flour
½ teaspoon baking powder
25 g/1 oz butter
7 ml/½ tablespoon caster sugar
½ beaten free-range egg
22 ml/1½ tablespoons milk

Skin the peaches (score the skins into four, then plunge them into boiling water to make this easier), stone them and slice thinly. Place the prepared peaches in a pan over a low heat and cook gently until the juices begin to bubble. Remove from the heat, allow to cool and drain the peaches, reserving the juice. Stir the sugar, spices and lemon juice into the reserved juice. Place the poached peach slices and the blueberries with the spiced juice in an ovenproof dish.

To make the topping, sift together the flour and baking powder and rub in the butter. Stir in the sugar. Mix the egg and milk together and stir into the flour mixture to form a dough. Roll out the dough on a floured board and cut into small rounds. Place the rounds on top of the fruit, brush with milk and bake in an oven preheated to 400°F (200°C) Gas Mark 6 for 20 minutes, or until golden brown. Serve with Greek yoghurt or custard.

Mixed Fruit Compote

This is lovely served with yoghurt for breakfast, or as a pudding with custard or ice cream. It will keep for 3–4 days in the refrigerator.

MAKES 8 PORTIONS

25 g/1 oz dried pears
25 g/1 oz stoned dried prunes
90 g/3½ oz dried peaches
90 g/3½ oz dried apple rings
25 g/1 oz dried banana flakes

25 g/1 oz sultanas
350 ml/12 fl oz orange juice
3 cloves
2.5 cm/1 in piece cinnamon stick
1 teaspoon grated orange zest

Place all the ingredients in a pan with 120 ml/4 fl oz water, bring to the boil, cover and simmer until all the fruits are very tender. Remove the cloves and cinnamon, and allow to cool. Chill until required.

Baked Egg Custard

Egg custard is another classic dish that is perennially popular with babies. I have used apricot spread in this recipe, but strawberry spread is equally good.

MAKES 4 PORTIONS

1 dessertspoon caster sugar
2 free-range eggs

300 ml/½ pint milk
2 tablespoons sugar-free apricot spread

Beat the sugar and eggs together until the sugar is dissolved and the mixture frothy. Whisk in the milk and apricot spread. Strain the mixture into a buttered ovenproof dish. Bake in an oven preheated to 300°F (150°C) Gas Mark 2 for 30 minutes, or until set. Allow to cool. Chill until required.

Mango, Kiwi & Papaya Fruit Salad

Exotic fruits are naturally high in fructose, vitamins and minerals, so they are a valuable addition to your baby's diet.

MAKES 8 PORTIONS

juice of 1 large orange
1 very ripe mango, peeled, stoned and chopped

2 kiwi fruit, peeled, sliced and quartered
1 ripe papaya, peeled, seeded and chopped

Pour the orange juice over the prepared mango, kiwi fruit and papaya. Serve with yoghurt, custard or ice cream.

Home-made Yoghurt

Natural yoghurt is an invaluable baby food, both on its own and as an ingredient in other dishes. Making your own is both cheap and easy, as well as being a good way of using up a surfeit of milk, if, like me, you are never sufficiently organised to leave a note for the milkman. The natural yoghurt used as a starter must be live.

MAKES ABOUT 600 ml/1 pint

550 ml/18 fl oz whole milk
1 tablespoon formula or ordinary

dried-milk powder
15 ml/1 tablespoon live natural yoghurt

Mix the milk with the powder and heat until almost boiling. Allow to cool until tepid. Whisk in the yoghurt and pour the mixture into a sterilised wide-necked vacuum flask. Leave for 6–8 hours. Transfer to a non-metallic container, cover and refrigerate for 6 hours. Use within a week.

NINE TO TWELVE MONTHS MENU CHART

This Menu Chart shows how you might integrate some of the recipes in this chapter into a balanced diet, which can be adapted for the rest of the family.

INGREDIENTS CHECKLIST

Apricot spread
Breads and muffins
Breakfast cereals
Bulghar wheat, pasta
  shapes, pearl
  barley, polenta
  and rice
Butterbeans, canned
Cannellini beans,
  canned
Cheese
Chickpeas, canned
Coconut, desiccated
Cream
Custard
Dried fruit
Eggs
Fresh fruit &
  vegetables
Fromage frais
Frozen vegetables
Fruit juices
Herbs and spices
Maple syrup
Mixed nuts
Oat bran
Oats
Passata
Peanut butter
Pear and apple
  spread
lentils, Puy and red
Sesame seeds
Sun-dried tomatoes
Tomatoes, canned
Tomato purée
Unsalted crisps
Yeast
Yoghurt, Greek

*Milk with breakfast
  and before mid-
  morning sleep each
  day.
**Juice with lunch, tea
  and supper.*

	Breakfast*	Lunch**	Tea	Supper	Bedtime
Day 1	Weetabix Banana Milk	Pasta with Three Pepper Pasta Sauce Fromage frais	Vegetable Crumble Mixed Fruit Compote Custard	Pumpkin & Apple Soup Sesame Breadsticks Oat Cookies	Milk
Day 2	Porridge with chopped apple	Vegetarian Shepherd's Pie Baked Egg Custard Fruit	Pasta with Mushroom & Four-cheese Pasta Sauce Mango, Kiwi & Papaya Fruit Salad	Maple Syrup-glazed Corn Avocado & Orange Salad Fromage frais	Milk
Day 3	Scrambled egg Toast soldiers Pear	Butterbean & Leek Gratin Green vegetables Fruit	Potato Hash Carrot Cake	Sandwiches Fromage frais	Milk
Day 4	Shreddies Strawberries Fromage frais	Lentil Moussaka Apple, Beetroot & Carrot Salad Rice Pudding	Hungarian Stuffed Marrow Fruit	Falafel with Minty Yoghurt Dip Fruit	Milk
Day 5	French Toast Apple Purée	Courgette, Cauliflower & Chickpea Curry Rice Fromage frais	Pasta with Spinach & Ricotta Sauce Fruit	Muffin Pizzas Baked Egg Custard	Milk
Day 6	Mixed Fruit Compote Yoghurt Toast	Lentil Hot Pot Vegetables Fruit	Cheese & Peanut Bites Apple Purée Rice Salad Blueberry & Peach Cobbler	Apollo Soup Cheese Straws Fromage frais	Milk
Day 7	Cornflakes Apple Toasted raisin bread	Pasta with Broccoli Pasta Sauce Strawberry Crunch	Barley Pot Fruit	Polenta with Tomato Sauce Apple & Raisin Muffins	Milk

CHAPTER FIVE

The Growing Gourmet

TODDLERS

From first birthday until starting school, your toddler will gain in independence and ability at an amazing rate. No longer a baby, he or she is now a determined participant in every aspect of daily life, and that includes meals. For parents, this stage can be tremendous fun, but it can also be frustrating when it comes to trying to ensure that a balanced diet is eaten. Food is no longer just fuel but an object of fascination to be explored, experimented with and only occasionally eaten. The important thing is to remain relaxed and keep the whole thing in perspective as your lovingly prepared, nutritionally sound supper ends up in your child's hair or on the carpet. Toddlers are quick to sense parental anxiety and even quicker to learn how to use this to manipulate parents to their own ends. Coax, cajole and encourage toddlers to eat, but never force them; otherwise the kitchen table will rapidly come to resemble a combat zone.

All children go through phases of faddy eating, picking at food, or sometimes not eating at all. However worrying these phases may be, do bear in mind that there are few recorded instances of toddlers who have succeeded in starving themselves to death before their fifth birthday. If children are of normal weight and height, then you can rest assured that they are consuming a few calories along with the fresh air you naïvely imagine sustains them. Toddlers have small tummies and even smaller attention spans, which means that it is physically difficult for them to eat enough at one meal to keep them going through until the next, and almost impossible for them to concentrate on the job once the initial hunger pangs have been satisfied. By all means work at introducing them to the concept of three meals a day, but don't expect them to get it for a good few years, and be prepared for a certain amount of between-meals grazing.

HEALTHY EATING HABITS

What toddlers eat, rather than when and how much, is what really matters. Experts now agree that eating habits and food preferences learned in childhood play a significant role in preventing the degenerative diseases that plague us in later life. Although vegetarians have a head start in meeting the dietary targets established by the World Health Organization, I have met more than one vegetarian child whose diet consists almost entirely of crisps, cola, chips and pizza. One mother, whose three-year-old was a regular teatime visitor,

apologetically warned me that her son would eat only spaghetti shapes and chips. As Dr Christopher Green, author of the excellent *Toddler Taming* (Vermilion) drily comments on such restricted diets: 'Is this mother telling me that junior gets up in the morning, takes the keys of the Volvo, drives down to the supermarket, loads up a trolley with chips and chocolate, drives home and eats them?'

Broadly speaking, you should try to make sure that your toddler eats plenty of fruit and vegetables, full-fat dairy products (small people actually need, rather than crave, those extra calories) and complex carbohydrates (bread and cereals). Try to restrict the intake of sweetened and refined foods such as cakes and biscuits, and keep salt to a minimum. However, don't be over-zealous in enforcing these ground rules – the occasional chocolate bar or chip is an indulgence, not a poison. Nor on any account should you attempt to feed your toddler a high-fibre, low-fat diet. This could lead to what doctors now disparagingly diagnose as 'Muesli-Belt Syndrome', a form of malnutrition experienced by a number of children whose parents force-feed them high-fibre 'hamster food' including large amounts of unrefined foods such as wholemeal bread, brown rice and brown pasta, in the erroneous belief that it is good for them. Toddlers need filling up with nutrients, not sawdust.

FOOD AS FUN

For toddlers, just as much as for adults, food should be a pleasure, not a chore. Variety is the key to stimulating a sense of enjoyment around food and mealtimes. If you feed your child a monotonous diet, eating will become a bore and your toddler will grow increasingly suspicious of new and unfamiliar foods. Small children can be amazingly adventurous in their tastes, if they are given the opportunity. From the age of one, the only dietary restriction that applies is the avoidance of whole nuts, because of the very real risk of choking. Otherwise, the supermarket is your toddler's oyster.

Like adults, toddlers eat first with their eyes, so food should look appealing and be attractively presented. There is no need to go to the extremes of carving tomato roses or radish fans, but a bowl of grey-looking mush is not going to do much to stimulate a reluctant appetite, whereas bright colours, interesting shapes and different textures will. A fruit salad, for example, will have far more toddler appeal if the fruits are prepared individually and arranged in a pattern on a plate rather than being presented as a bowl of homogenous lumps. A simple salad of grated carrot and apple will entrance with its contrasting colours. Keep portions small so as not to overwhelm. You can always add more if the first portion disappears quickly.

From a very early age, most children are fascinated by food preparation. When time, patience and safety considerations permit, allow your child to help. My son's idea of a perfect Sunday morning is to be allowed to stand on a chair next to me, popping pea pods or spreading tomato sauce on pizza bases. For a special treat, we make chocolate rice crispy cakes for him to take to nursery on Monday. The pride with which he bears those misshapen mountains to his classmates makes all the mess worthwhile. Handling food helps him to feel involved – even if this consists simply of selecting the pasta shapes which he wants to accompany his sauce.

Up until their first birthday, most children are quite happy to allow parents to feed them, but increasing independence inevitably leads to the insistence on doing it themselves. Grit your teeth, protect your carpets, keep a damp flannel handy and resist the temptation to intervene too much. It's worth investing in a set of special cutlery with chunky, toddler-friendly handles to aid the process. At first it will be slow and messy but, as your child's dexterity increases, more of the food will eventually reach its intended destination and satisfaction and confidence will be gained from having managed alone.

Shared family meals are an ideal which is not always possible or practical, given the demands of modern life. On those occasions when it is necessary for your toddler to eat independently, try to avoid the temptation to plonk him or her in front of the electronic babysitter (TV). Instead, make an occasion of the affair by preparing a picnic to be shared with inanimate friends in the garden, or make a play tent with a clothes airer and old blanket for pretend camping. My son especially enjoys snacking 'at sea', pretending he is afloat in his old baby bath.

A TIME FOR TOGETHERNESS

As parents, in our eagerness to ensure that our toddlers consume enough of the right foods to maintain healthy growth, it is easy to lose sight of the fact that food performs a key role in the bonding process. Providing wholesome, home-cooked food is in itself an expression of our care for those we love. Mealtimes should be a social event; they are often the only times when the family can sit down together and exchange news and ideas in a relaxed, unhurried atmosphere. Even before children are able to join in conversation, they can learn to appreciate this special time together. And, never underestimate the power of food as education. Much of my son's knowledge of different countries and ways of life has been inspired by discussions stemming from the food on his plate. Another plus point is that children who regularly eat with adults tend to have fewer problems grasping the rudiments of table manners – example is better than instruction. Also, most children really enjoy eating out, with its sense of occasion. Italian and Chinese restaurants are good first choices, as the waiters often have a relaxed attitude to small people and will make a great fuss of diminutive customers.

By the age of two or so many toddlers will be attending a toddler group or nursery and developing a social life of their own. Encourage this by inviting little friends for teatime play sessions and giving the food a party feel (there are lots of suggestions for suitable menus at the end of this chapter). Children who learn at an early age to relate to their peers and to share find it much easier to cope when the time comes to start school.

ABOUT THE RECIPES

The recipes in this section are designed to introduce your toddler to as wide a variety of tastes and textures as possible while still appealing to the rest of the family. In the early days you may find that you need to be a little cautious with the flavourings and seasonings, but by the time your toddler is three or four there should be no reason to modify the recipes, providing that you yourself do not have an embarrassing sodium habit or a penchant for fiery curries. By introducing your toddler to delicious, wholesome food at an early age you are making one of the greatest investments possible in your child's future health and happiness. Bon *appetit.*

SOUPS, SANDWICHES & SNACKS

Four Seasons Soup

This colourful, nutritious soup is an ideal way of introducing toddlers to vegetable chunks. Let them use pieces of crusty bread to fish out the different vegetables, and see how many they recognise.

MAKES 4 ADULT PORTIONS

15 ml/1 tablespoon olive oil
1 onion, finely chopped
1 parsnip, peeled and chopped
225 g/8 oz swede, diced
225 g/8 oz potato, diced
1 teaspoon dried mixed herbs (optional)

30 ml/2 tablespoons tomato purée
600 ml/1 pint light
vegetable stock
1 courgette, diced
75 g/3 oz frozen peas
salt and black pepper to taste

Heat the oil, add the onion, parsnip, swede and potato and cook gently, without colouring, for 5 minutes. Add the herbs, tomato purée and stock, bring to the boil, cover and simmer for 25 minutes. Add the diced courgette and peas. Season, cover and simmer for a further 5–10 minutes.

Beetroot & Apple Soup

Toddlers love colourful food so the deep, rich hue of this sweet and satisfying soup is highly appealing. My son calls it 'lipstick soup' because of the slight stain it leaves around the mouths of messy eaters!

MAKES 4 ADULT PORTIONS

15 ml/1 tablespoon olive oil
2 medium raw beetroots, peeled and diced
1 cooking apple, peeled, cored and chopped
1 medium potato, grated

500 ml/16 fl oz light vegetable stock
150 ml/5 fl oz apple juice
60 ml/4 tablespoons Greek yoghurt
salt and black pepper to taste

Heat the oil, add the beetroot and apple and fry gently for 3–4 minutes. Add the potato and stock, bring to the boil, cover and simmer for 30 minutes, or until the beetroot is tender. Cool slightly, then add the apple juice and blend in a liquidiser until smooth. Reheat, season to taste and serve with a swirl of Greek yoghurt.

Carrot & Orange Soup

This became a favourite with my son on a skiing holiday in France, during which the vegetarians in the party received carrot soup and an omelette at every meal. Nowadays, we have it less frequently, served with fingers of warmed pitta bread or crunchy garlic croutons.

MAKES 4 ADULT PORTIONS

15 ml/1 tablespoon olive oil
1 onion, finely chopped
750 g/1½ lb carrots, washed and diced
grated rind and juice of 1 orange

500 ml/16 fl oz light vegetable stock
150 ml/5 fl oz milk
salt and black pepper to taste

Heat the oil, add the onion and carrots, cover and cook gently for 5–10 minutes. Add the orange rind and juice, and the stock, bring to the boil and simmer for 20 minutes or until the carrots are tender. Cool slightly, add the milk and blend in a liquidiser. Reheat and season to taste.

Sandwiches

Sandwiches make terrific toddler food as they can be enjoyed without parental intervention. They also offer great scope for ingenuity. Try using different breads (though anything with seeds is best avoided), making pinwheels or shapes using pastry cutters, or even using white and brown bread to make stripy sandwiches. Reluctant eaters can usually be coaxed by the prospect of a picnic, even if it is in the sitting room, so, to ensure trouble-free teas, it's worth investing in a lunch box featuring your child's favourite cartoon character. I have found the following fillings to be particularly successful .

CREAM CHEESE & HONEY FACES

MAKES 4 MINI SANDWICHES

2 slices wholemeal bread, lightly buttered
30 ml/2 tablespoons cream cheese
15 ml/1 tablespoon runny honey
handful of raisins

Spread the bread with the cheese and honey, and sandwich together. Remove the crusts and stamp out four small rounds using a cocktail pastry cutter. Stud with raisins to make eyes, noses and mouths.

PEANUT BUTTER & BANANA FINGERS

MAKES 3 FINGERS

1 slice each white and brown bread, buttered
15 ml/1 tablespoon smooth peanut butter
1 small banana, mashed

Spread the white bread with the peanut butter, and top with mashed banana. Cover with the brown bread. Cut off the crusts and cut into three fingers.

CARROT & HUMMUS POCKETS

MAKES 2 MINI PITTAS

2 mini pitta breads
45 ml/3 tablespoons hummus (see page 40)
1 small carrot, grated

Warm the pitta breads and split lengthways. Mix together the hummus and grated carrot and use the mixture to fill the pitta bread.

BRIE & BLACK GRAPE

MAKES 4

2 slices fruited tea bread, lightly buttered
50 g/2 oz ripe Brie cheese, sliced
4 black grapes, halved and seeded

Arrange the Brie on one slice of the bread. Top with the grape halves and cover with the remaining slice of bread. Cut off the crusts and cut into quarters.

ITALIAN FLAG ROLLS

MAKES 4 ROLLS

4 soft white mini rolls, split and buttered
1 small avocado, peeled, stoned and mashed
2 tomatoes, thinly sliced
salt and black pepper to taste
4 slices mozzarella cheese

Divide the avocado and tomato among the rolls and season lightly. Top with a slice of mozzarella cheese.

BOURSIN & BEAN SLICES

MAKES 4

4 slices French bread
2 tablespoons Boursin cheese
2 tablespoons canned red kidney beans,
rinsed and drained

Mash together the Boursin cheese and kidney beans. Spread evenly over the slices of French bread.

Baked Potato

Baked potatoes are another great toddler food, but the key to their acceptance is to get the potato fluffy and light and the skin deliciously crunchy. Sadly, speedy though they may be, microwave ovens cannot achieve this. You need to boil the potatoes for 20 minutes before transferring them to a hot oven, 400°F (200°C) Gas Mark 6, for about 20–30 minutes, depending on size. Then split the potatoes, scoop out the flesh, mash the flesh with a little butter, pile it back into the skins and fill the potatoes with any of the following suggestions.

CREAM CHEESE & CHIVES

FOR 2 POTATOES

100 g/4 oz cream cheese
1 tablespoon chopped chives

Mix together the cheese and chives and spoon into two prepared potatoes.

BEEFLESS BOLOGNESE

See the recipe for Beefless Bolognese sauce on page 113. The leftover sauce is ideal as a potato filling. Sprinkle grated pecorino cheese over the top before serving.

CREAMY MUSHROOMS

FOR 2 POTATOES

25 g/1 oz butter
100 g/4 oz button mushrooms, wiped and sliced
1 tablespoon flour
300 ml/½ pint milk
salt and black pepper to taste
grated nutmeg to taste

Heat the butter and gently fry the mushrooms until soft. Sprinkle the flour on to the mushrooms and cook, stirring, for 1–2 minutes. Incorporate the milk gradually. Bring to the boil, simmer for 1 minute and add seasoning and nutmeg to taste. Spoon the creamy mushrooms into two prepared potatoes, and serve with green salad.

BEANFEAST

FOR 2 POTATOES

200 g/7 oz can baked beans
50 g/2 oz Cheddar cheese, grated
black pepper
dash of vegetarian Worcestershire sauce

Heat the beans and stir in the cheese. Season with pepper and Worcestershire sauce. Spoon into two prepared potatoes.

GREEN & GOLD

FOR 2 POTATOES

50 g/2 oz frozen peas
50 g/2 oz frozen sweetcorn
100 g/4 oz cottage cheese
salt and black pepper to taste

Cook the peas and sweetcorn according to the directions on their packets. Drain the cooked vegetables and mix them with the cottage cheese. Season to taste and spoon into two prepared potatoes.

RATATOUILLE

See the recipe for Ratatouille on page 53, and use to fill prepared potatoes.

Cheese & Herb Scones

These scones are super with soup for lunch or as a teatime extra, but my son especially likes them for breakfast.

MAKES 24 MINI SCONES

225 g/8 oz wholemeal self-raising flour
pinch of salt
1 teaspoon dried mustard powder
1 teaspoon baking powder
1 teaspoon dried mixed herbs

40 g/1½ oz butter
100 g/4 oz Cheddar cheese, grated
150 ml/5 fl oz milk, plus a little extra
for brushing

Sift together the flour, salt, mustard, baking powder and herbs. Rub in the butter. Stir in half the cheese and work to a soft dough with the milk. Turn the mixture on to a lightly floured board and knead gently. Roll out to a thickness of approximately 2.5 cm/1 in and cut into rounds. Sprinkle the remaining cheese over the top. Bake on an oiled baking sheet in an oven preheated to 425°F (220°C) Gas Mark 7 for 10 minutes, or until the scones sound hollow when tapped underneath. Cool on a wire rack.

Muffin Rabbits

To toddlers, rarebit and rabbit are easily confused words and I have never had the heart to explain the difference to my son. Hence, I always serve this teatime staple cut into 'ears', that is, halves.

MAKES 4

1 *muffin, split*
a little Marmite or Vegemite
15 g/½ oz butter

2 *spring onions, finely chopped*
50 g/2 oz Cheddar cheese, grated
a little milk

Toast the muffin lightly and spread thinly with Marmite or Vegemite. Melt the butter, add the spring onions and fry gently until softened. Stir in the cheese, adding a little milk to give a smooth consistency and, when the mixture is creamy, spread it on the muffin. Cut the muffin into halves and serve with tomato ketchup.

Potato Cakes

These are wonderful for both breakfast and tea, served either German-style, with apple sauce, or more conventionally with grilled tomatoes and mushrooms.

MAKES 8

450 g/1 lb mashed potato
100 g/4 oz plain flour
100 g/4 oz melted butter

salt and black pepper to taste
chopped parsley to taste
butter for frying

Mash together the potato and flour. Work in the melted butter, seasoning and parsley. Shape the dough into little cakes of approximately 3.5 cm/1½ in diameter. Heat a little butter in a large frying pan. When the butter is sizzling, add the potato cakes and cook for 5–7 minutes on both sides, or until golden brown. Serve immediately.

☺	☹

Frittata

Most toddlers adore omelettes, which makes them the ideal vehicle for introducing different vegetables. Krishnan calls this 'breakfast supper' because of its similarity to scrambled eggs.

MAKES 4 ADULT PORTIONS

15 ml/1 tablespoon olive oil
4 courgettes, sliced
1 red pepper, seeded and chopped
1 medium potato, boiled and diced
1 clove garlic, finely chopped

1 bunch of spring onions, finely chopped
1 tablespoon chopped basil
1 tablespoon chopped parsley
salt and black pepper to taste
6 free-range eggs, beaten

Heat the oil in a large frying pan, add the courgettes and pepper and cook gently until soft. Stir in the potato and garlic. Add the onions, herbs and seasoning to the eggs. Pour the egg mixture over the vegetables in the frying pan. Cook gently until golden underneath. Place the pan under a preheated grill until the top of the frittata is brown. Serve, hot or cold, cut into wedges.

☺	☹

Pasta Salad

A lot of toddlers, my own included, are unenthusiastic about salads, but if you include their preferred ingredients, like pasta, they won't even notice they are eating salad.

MAKES 4 ADULT PORTIONS

225 g/8 oz (dry weight) pasta shapes, cooked
1 red pepper, seeded and finely chopped
1 green pepper, seeded and finely chopped
100 g/4 oz canned sweetcorn

100 g/4 oz cooked frozen peas
2 tomatoes, skinned, seeded and chopped
45 ml/3 tablespoons olive oil
salt and black pepper to taste

Mix together the pasta and all the prepared vegetables in a bowl. Add the olive oil, season to taste and toss lightly.

Three-colour Salad

This scaled-down version of the classic *insalata tricolore* has the bright colours, mild flavours and creamy textures which appeal to most children.

MAKES 4 ADULT PORTIONS

225 g/8 oz cherry tomatoes, quartered
1 medium avocado, peeled, stoned
and chopped

150 g/5 oz mozzarella cheese, cubed
30 ml/2 tablespoons olive oil
salt and black pepper to taste

Mix together the tomatoes, avocado and cheese. Pour the olive oil over the salad, season to taste and serve with crunchy bread.

Curried Rice Salad

This slightly spicy, sweet and nutritious salad is an excellent accompaniment to grilled tofu kebabs or burgers.

MAKES 6 ADULT PORTIONS

225 g/8 oz basmati rice
1 teaspoon turmeric
salt
400 g/14 oz can green lentils, drained
100 g/4 oz peas, cooked
100 g/4 oz baby spinach, washed, stalks removed, and finely sliced

DRESSING
60 ml/4 tablespoons olive oil
15 ml/1 tablespoon soy sauce
15 ml/1 tablespoon mango chutney
½ teaspoon mild curry powder

Cook the basmati rice in water, until tender, adding the turmeric and salt to taste. Stir in the lentils, peas and spinach. Mix together the dressing ingredients. Pour the dressing over the salad and toss. Chill.

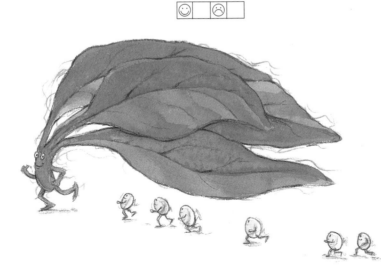

Garlic Bread

Any preconceptions you may have about toddlers not liking garlic will disappear when you confront them with a plate of garlic bread. For a more nutritious snack, try adding a little grated cheese to the butter mix.

FOR 1 BAGUETTE

1 *small baguette (French bread)*
75 g/3 oz softened butter
1 teaspoon chopped parsley

2 *cloves garlic, very finely chopped*
salt and black pepper to taste

Slice the baguette, but do not cut completely through. Mix the butter, parsley and garlic together and season to taste. Spread the mixture on to the cut surfaces of the bread, wrap the baguette in foil and place in a hot oven 400°F (200°C) Gas Mark 6 for 10–15 minutes, or until the butter is melted and the crust crisp.

MAIN COURSES

Beefless Bolognese

I've yet to come across a child who isn't enthusiastic about this tasty sauce, whether it is served with pasta, or in shepherd's pie or as a filling for baked potatoes. The quantity is rather generous because it makes an excellent freezer standby.

MAKES 8 ADULT PORTIONS

60 ml/4 tablespoons olive oil
1 large onion, chopped
2 cloves garlic, crushed
1 tablespoon chopped basil
scant teaspoon dried oregano
1 bay leaf
1 carrot, peeled and diced
1 stick celery, finely chopped
1 red pepper, seeded and chopped

175 g/6 oz button mushrooms, quartered
30 ml/2 tablespoons tomato purée
150 ml/5 fl oz red wine
15 ml/1 tablespoon dark soy sauce
salt and black pepper to taste
225 g/8 oz can chopped tomatoes
2 x 400 g/14 oz cans brown lentils, drained
1 tablespoon chopped flat-leaf parsley

Heat the oil, add the onion, garlic, basil, oregano and bay leaf and fry until the onions are transparent. Add the carrot, celery and red pepper, cook for a few minutes, then add the mushrooms. When the mushrooms begin to wilt, stir in the remaining ingredients, bring to the boil, cover and simmer for approximately 40 minutes. Allow to cool, transfer to a food processor and blend coarsely (if you prefer a chunkier texture blend only half the mixture). Before serving, reheat and check seasoning.

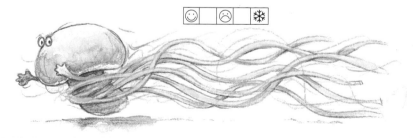

Spinach & Mushroom Lasagne

A nursery nature session on the subject of mushrooms left my son highly suspicious of all varieties of mushroom for some time. Such was his passion for this richly satisfying lasagne, however, that he conveniently overlooked their inclusion.

MAKES 6 ADULT PORTIONS

MUSHROOM SAUCE
25 g/1 oz butter
2 onions, peeled and chopped
225 g/8 oz mushrooms, wiped
and thinly sliced
2 cloves garlic, crushed
1 tablespoon chopped flat-leaf parsley
1 tablespoon chopped basil
60 ml/4 tablespoons tomato purée
400 g/14 oz can chopped tomatoes (replace
some juice with red wine for a richer sauce)
15 ml/1 tablespoon soy sauce
5 ml/1 teaspoon honey
salt and black pepper to taste

CHEESE SAUCE
40 g/1½ oz butter
40 g/1½ oz plain flour
450 ml/¾ pint milk
100 g/4 oz Cheddar cheese, grated
pinch of dry mustard powder
pinch of grated nutmeg

225 g/8 oz spinach lasagne (the type
requiring no precooking)
450 g/1 lb chopped frozen spinach,
defrosted and drained

For the mushroom sauce, melt the butter, and fry the onions until transparent. Add the mushrooms, garlic and herbs and continue frying gently. Stir in the tomato purée, tomatoes, soy sauce and honey. Season and simmer for 10 minutes.

Prepare the cheese sauce. Melt the butter, add the flour and cook, stirring, for 2–3 minutes. Gradually incorporate the milk. Allow the sauce to bubble for 1 minute, then turn off the heat and stir in half the grated cheese and the seasoning.

Grease a large ovenproof dish and layer the lasagne, cheese sauce, spinach and mushroom sauce, finishing with a layer of lasagne topped with cheese sauce. Sprinkle the remaining cheese on the top and bake in an oven preheated to 350°F (180°C) Gas Mark 4 for 40 minutes. Leave to stand for 10 minutes before serving.

Tomato & Mascarpone Pasta Sauce

This lovely creamy sauce goes well with any pasta. Let toddlers choose some of the specially designed children's pasta shapes now available, such as farm animals or Postman Pat, and you have a nutritious meal that's also fun to eat.

MAKES 4 ADULT PORTIONS

30 ml/2 tablespoons olive oil
1 onion, finely chopped
1 clove garlic, finely chopped
1 tablespoon chopped flat-leaf parsley
1 tablespoon chopped basil leaves

400 g/14 oz can chopped tomatoes
½ teaspoon honey
salt and black pepper to taste
225 g/8 oz mascarpone cheese

Heat the oil and gently fry the onion and garlic until very soft but not coloured. Stir in the herbs, fry for 1 minute, then add the tomatoes, honey and seasoning. Add 85 ml/3 fl oz water, bring to the boil and allow the sauce to bubble gently for 30 minutes. Stir in the mascarpone, heat through and check seasoning.

Treasure Island Couscous

When my son was still rather reluctant about lumps in food we used to pretend that the couscous in this recipe was the beach and that the vegetables were the treasure buried in the sand. The subterfuge worked beautifully.

MAKES 6 ADULT PORTIONS

30 ml/2 tablespoons olive oil, plus a little for the couscous
1 large onion, peeled and chopped
100 g/4 oz carrot, sliced
100 g/4 oz swede, cubed
1 clove garlic, finely chopped
½ teaspoon grated ginger
pinch of ground cinnamon
50 g/2 oz dried apricots, chopped
50 g/2 oz raisins

1 litre/1½ pints light vegetable stock
400 g/14 oz can chickpeas, drained
100 g/4 oz okra, wiped and sliced
1 courgette, sliced
350 g/12 oz couscous
50 g/2 oz butter
salt and black pepper to taste
1–2 tablespoons chopped coriander leaves (optional)

Heat the oil, add the onion, carrot and swede and fry gently for 10 minutes. Add the garlic, ginger and cinnamon and cook for 2 minutes. Now add the apricots and raisins, pour in the stock and simmer until the carrots are tender and the dried fruits plump, approximately 20 minutes. Add the chickpeas, okra and courgette and continue cooking for a further 10–15 minutes.

Meanwhile, prepare the couscous by placing 350 ml/12 fl oz of water in a pan. Add 1 teaspoon of salt and a little oil and bring to the boil. Remove from the heat, stir in the couscous and leave for 3 minutes, or until the couscous has absorbed the water. Stir in the butter and fluff up the grains using a fork.

Season the vegetables, sprinkle the coriander (if using) over them and serve on a bed of couscous.

Cauliflower & Potato Bake

This more substantial version of the perennially popular cauliflower cheese has a crunchy crisp topping to maximise its toddler-tempting power.

MAKES 6 ADULT PORTIONS

1 large cauliflower
40 g/1½ oz butter
450 g/1 lb waxy new potatoes, cooked
and sliced
100 g/4 oz Gruyère cheese, grated

salt and black pepper to taste
2 free-range eggs, beaten
50 ml/2 fl oz Greek yoghurt
40 g/1½ oz reduced-fat plain crisps,
finely crushed

Break the cauliflower into florets and steam them until just tender. Generously butter an ovenproof gratin dish and layer into it the cauliflower, potatoes and grated cheese, lightly seasoning each layer with salt and pepper. Finish with a layer of cheese. Mix together the beaten eggs and yoghurt, spoon this over the cheese and sprinkle the crushed crisps on the top. Bake in an oven preheated to 400°F (200°C) Gas Mark 6 for 30 minutes, or until golden brown and bubbling.

Frosty Stew

My son calls this hearty, homely dish 'Frosty Stew' because it only appears on bitterly cold days. For younger toddlers, lightly mash the vegetable chunks. Try serving it with creamy mashed potatoes or herby dumplings, perfect for keeping out the cold.

MAKES 4 ADULT PORTIONS

60 ml/4 tablespoons vegetable oil
350 g/12 oz baby onions, peeled
1 clove garlic, crushed
2 sticks celery, sliced
2 large carrots, peeled and cut into chunks
2 large parsnips, peeled and cut into chunks
225 g/8 oz pumpkin flesh, cubed
25 g/1 oz plain flour
300 ml/½ pint vegetable stock

275 ml/9 fl oz dark beer
15 ml/1 tablespoon vegetarian
Worcestershire sauce
2 tablespoons chopped flat-leaf parsley
2 bay leaves
1 bouquet garni
30 ml/2 tablespoons tomato purée
salt and black pepper to taste

Heat the oil in a large flameproof casserole and fry the onions, garlic and celery until golden. Add the remaining vegetables and continue frying until they are lightly browned. Sprinkle the flour over the vegetables and stir well to incorporate. Add the stock, beer, Worcestershire sauce, herbs and tomato purée. Season to taste and bring to the boil, stirring. Cover and cook in an oven preheated to 350°F (180°C) Gas Mark 4 for about 45 minutes, or until all the vegetables are tender.

Bread & Cheese Pudding

A savoury version of the nursery favourite, bread and butter pudding (see page 130), this is delicious with a salad of sweet cherry tomatoes.

MAKES 4 ADULT PORTIONS

25 g/1 oz butter, plus a little for spreading
1 large leek, very finely chopped
½ teaspoon dried thyme
100 g/4 oz strong Cheddar cheese, grated
75 g/3 oz Parmesan cheese, grated
½ teaspoon dried mustard powder

1 tablespoon chopped chives (optional)
8 medium slices white bread, crusts removed
3 free-range eggs
500 ml/16 fl oz milk
salt and black pepper to taste

Heat the butter in a frying pan, add the leek and thyme and cook slowly for approximately 20 minutes, until soft and golden. Mix together the cheeses, mustard and chives. Lightly butter the bread and a large ovenproof dish. Place four slices of the bread in a single layer in the base of the dish, spread with the leek mixture and sprinkle half the cheese over the top. Place the remaining bread and cheese on top. Beat together the eggs and milk, season lightly and pour this mixture over the bread and cheese. Leave to stand for 30 minutes, then bake at 375°F (190°C) Gas Mark 5 for 30 minutes, or until golden and risen.

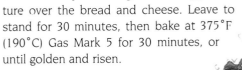

Wild West Beans

All children love baked beans so the commercial brands (especially the low salt and sugar varieties) are an excellent standby. However, it is fun to make your own version when time permits.

MAKES 6–8 ADULT PORTIONS

15 ml/1 tablespoon olive oil
½ onion, peeled and finely chopped
1 clove garlic, peeled and crushed
200g/7 oz can chopped tomatoes
30 ml/2 tablespoons soy sauce
150 ml/5 fl oz apple juice

30 ml/2 tablespoons molasses
dash of vegetarian Worcestershire sauce
15 ml/1 tablespoon French mustard
salt and black pepper to taste
2 x 400g/14 oz cans haricot beans, drained

Heat the oil in a saucepan, add the onion and garlic, and sweat until softened. Stir in the tomatoes, soy sauce, apple juice, molasses, Worcestershire sauce and mustard. Bring to the boil and simmer for 10–15 minutes, or until the liquid is slightly reduced. Add the drained beans and simmer for 20–30 minutes. Season and serve with Mini Glamorgan Sausages (see page 135), jacket potatoes, vegetarian hot dogs or home-made Mini Veggie Burgers (see page 136).

Vegetarian Sausage &
Apple Casserole

Like most children, my son loves sweet and sour taste combinations, so this wholesome casserole devised by my friend Heather Mairs, Director of The Vegetarian Society Cookery School, is a real hit. Any of the excellent proprietary brands of vegetarian sausage now on the market can be used. For a special treat, try serving this piled into individual Yorkshire puddings.

MAKES 4–6 ADULT PORTIONS

1 *packet vegetarian sausages (about 8)*
750 *g/1½ lb waxy potatoes, peeled and cubed*
30 *ml/2 tablespoons vegetable oil*
1 *large onion, peeled and finely chopped*
2 *cloves garlic, crushed*
1 *bay leaf*
2 *teaspoons dried thyme*

450 *g/1 lb carrots, sliced*
1 *large cooking apple, peeled, cored and cubed*
400g/14 *oz can chopped tomatoes*
300 *ml/½ pint apple juice or cider*
15 *ml/1 tablespoon tomato purée*
salt and black pepper to taste

Grill the sausages until brown, chop them into chunks and set aside. Boil the potatoes in salted water for 5 minutes and drain. Heat the oil, fry the onion gently until soft, then add the garlic and herbs and continue frying for 2 minutes. Add the carrots and apple and fry for a further 5 minutes. Stir in the tomatoes, apple juice or cider, and tomato purée. Bring to the boil and simmer for 15 minutes. Finally add the potatoes and sausages to the tomato mixture, season and simmer for 10–15 minutes.

Prehistoric Potato Hash

My father, a Lancashire lad and committed carnivore, believed that a child deprived of 'tater hash' was a child denied one of life's great pleasures. To convince him that his non-meat-eating grandson was not going to grow up underprivileged, I devised this vegetarian version for them both to enjoy. Though ridiculously simple, it works.

MAKES 4–6 ADULT PORTIONS

450 g/1 lb Realeat Vegesteak
1 large onion, peeled and chopped
1 large carrot, peeled and diced
750 g/1½ lb floury potatoes, peeled and cubed

salt and black pepper to taste
vegetable stock
225 g/8 oz shortcrust pastry
1 free-range egg, beaten

Place the Vegesteak along with the prepared vegetables in a deep earthenware dish, season and pour over sufficient stock to cover the contents. Cover and cook in an oven preheated to 350°F (180°C) Gas Mark 4 for approximately 1½–2 hours. Remove from the oven and raise the oven temperature to 400°F (200°C) Gas Mark 6. Roll out the pastry to form a lid for the dish, using the trimmings to make dinosaur shapes to decorate. Glaze with the beaten egg and return to the oven for 15–20 minutes, or until golden brown. Serve with steamed cabbage.

Stir-fried Vegetables

Even children who are particularly picky about vegetables seem to love them stir-fried. Vary the combinations according to what is in season and your child's preferences. I find that baby sweetcorn, broccoli, mushrooms, courgettes and peppers all work well. Also, this is one of the few ways that lettuce becomes acceptable to small children.

MAKES 6 ADULT PORTIONS

MARINADE
30 ml/2 tablespoons soy sauce
grated rind and juice of 1 orange
1 clove garlic, crushed
15 ml/1 tablespoon honey

225 g/8 oz cubed tofu
30 ml/2 tablespoons vegetable oil
few drops sesame oil

2 cloves garlic, finely chopped
bunch of spring onions, finely sliced
1 kg/2 lb prepared mixed vegetables: carrots,
red and green peppers, broccoli, baby
sweetcorn, courgettes, lettuce
100 g/4 oz almond halves or cashew nuts
15 ml/1 tablespoon soy sauce
15 ml/1 tablespoon mirin (Chinese rice
wine) or sherry

Mix together the soy sauce, orange rind and juice, garlic and honey, and stir in the cubed tofu. Leave to marinate for at least 1 hour. Heat the oil in a wok or large frying pan. Stir-fry the marinated tofu for 2–3 minutes, remove from the oil and drain on kitchen paper.

Fry the garlic and onions in the wok for 1–2 minutes. Add the vegetables according to the length of time they need to cook: carrots and peppers first, courgettes second, and lettuce last. Stir-fry until cooked through but still crisp.

Meanwhile, finely chop or grind the nuts, then dry-fry them in a separate pan until golden. Add the soy sauce, mirin or sherry, and tofu to the vegetables and stir briskly. Scatter the nuts over the vegetables, and serve with boiled rice.

Paella

Although the list of ingredients does seem rather daunting, this paella is extremely easy to prepare and ranks among my son's 'best-ever dinners'. Omit the olives if your toddler hasn't yet acquired the taste – in our house they always disappear first.

MAKES 8 ADULT PORTIONS

30 ml/2 tablespoons olive oil
1 onion, peeled and chopped
2 cloves garlic, peeled and chopped
1 red pepper, seeded and chopped
1 green pepper, seeded and chopped
1 bay leaf
1 beef tomato, peeled, seeded and chopped
50 g/2 oz butter
400 g/14 oz arborio rice
1 litre/1½ pints light vegetable stock mixed with white wine

½ teaspoon paprika
1 teaspoon turmeric
salt and black pepper to taste
1 packet vegetarian frankfurters
100 g/4 oz frozen peas
100 g/4 oz frozen sweetcorn
100 g/4 oz button mushrooms
50 g/2 oz black olives (optional)
chopped flat-leaf parsley and lemon wedges to serve

Heat the oil in a wok, add the onion, garlic, peppers and bay leaf, and fry gently for 5 minutes. Stir in the tomato, then the butter and, when bubbling, stir in the rice, making sure that it is thoroughly coated with butter.

In another pan, heat the stock and wine, mixing in the paprika, turmeric and seasoning. When the rice is opaque, pour the liquid on to it, stir well and bring to the boil. Reduce the heat, cover tightly and simmer gently for 20 minutes without removing the lid. Meanwhile, cook the sausages according to the instructions on the packet and cut them into chunks. Add the sausages and all remaining ingredients to the rice, cover and cook for a further 10–15 minutes. To serve, scatter chopped parsley on top, and decorate with lemon wedges.

Vegetable Curry

The creamy sweetness of the coconut milk makes this curry appeal to even the most timid of palates, especially when accompanied by pappadums ('big crisps, Mummy'), slices of banana and natural yoghurt.

MAKES 4 ADULT PORTIONS

15 ml/1 tablespoon vegetable oil
1 onion, peeled and finely chopped
1 clove garlic, chopped
15 ml/1 tablespoon mild curry powder
1 kg/2 lb prepared vegetables: carrots,

potatoes, cauliflower and green beans
300 ml/½ pint canned coconut milk
salt and black pepper to taste
100 g/4 oz frozen peas
150 ml/5 fl oz natural yoghurt

Heat the oil, add the onion and garlic and fry until soft. Stir in the curry powder and cook for 1–2 minutes. Add the prepared vegetables and fry for a few minutes, stirring to coat them with the spices. Pour on the coconut milk (add a little extra water if necessary), cover and simmer gently until the vegetables are almost tender (about 20 minutes). Season, add the frozen peas and cook for a further 15 minutes. Stir in the yoghurt, heat through and serve on a bed of boiled rice.

Leek Tart

Caramelised leeks give this savoury tart a slight sweetness which all children love. Salad makes a good accompaniment.

MAKES 6 ADULT PORTIONS

225 g/8 oz shortcrust pastry
50 g/2 oz butter
450 g/1 lb leeks, trimmed, washed and
finely chopped
25 g/1 oz plain flour

300 ml/½ pint milk
75 g/3 oz Cheddar cheese, grated
2 free-range eggs, beaten
salt and black pepper to taste
grated nutmeg to taste

Roll out the pastry and use to line an oiled 23 cm/9 in flan tin. Melt half the butter in a pan, add the leeks, cover and cook gently for 20 minutes, until soft and golden. Meanwhile, in another pan, melt the remaining butter, stir in the flour and cook, without allowing it to colour, for 1–2 minutes. Heat the milk, then gradually beat it into the flour mixture until you have a smooth sauce. Simmer for 1–2 minutes. Now stir the leeks, cheese, beaten egg, seasoning and nutmeg into the sauce. Pour the mixture into the pastry case and bake in an oven preheated to 375°F (190°C) Gas Mark 5 for 30–35 minutes, until golden brown and risen.

SWEET TREATS

Thomas' Lemon Flan

My son's godmother, Anne Lawman, used to make this quick, cheesecake-like pudding for her own grandson, and now it's a firm favourite with my son, too. If the mixture does not thicken, add a little more lemon juice.

MAKES 8–10 ADULT PORTIONS

50 g/2 oz butter
25 g/1 oz demerara sugar
100 g/4 oz digestive biscuits (Graham crackers), crushed

300 ml/½ pint double cream
400 g/14 oz can condensed milk
grated rind and juice of 2 large lemons
green grapes to decorate

Melt the butter, add the sugar and stir in the biscuit crumbs. Press this mixture into the base and sides of a 20 cm/8 in flan tin. Place the cream, condensed milk, lemon rind and juice in a large bowl and whisk until well blended and slightly thickened. Pour the mixture into the biscuit base and chill until set (at least 3 hours) before decorating with grapes.

☺ ☹

Chocolate Baked Bananas

My son, in common with most small children, is passionately fond of both bananas and chocolate. This unusual recipe makes a little chocolate go a long way, which keeps us both happy.

MAKES 4 ADULT PORTIONS

4 *large bananas, unpeeled*
100 *g/4 oz milk or plain chocolate, chopped*

4 *teaspoons mixed nuts, finely chopped, or ground*

Trim the ends of the bananas, but do not peel. Wipe the skins and split the bananas lengthways, but not through the skin underneath. Press the chopped chocolate into the split of each banana, then wrap them tightly (individually) in foil. Bake in an oven preheated to 400°F (200°C) Gas Mark 6 for 25 minutes, or until the banana skins are blackened and the flesh soft. Sprinkle the chopped nuts over the chocolate filling and serve. Your toddler will enjoy scooping the delicious sticky mixture directly out of the skin.

Raspberry Trifle

Fresh raspberries can be a little tart for toddlers' tastes but the jelly and sponge offset this. For a change, try making this in individual glass sundae dishes, or with strawberries and strawberry jelly.

MAKES 6 ADULT PORTIONS

1 *raspberry-jam-filled Swiss roll*
225 *g/8 oz raspberries, washed and hulled*
1 *packet vegetarian raspberry jelly crystals*
(from health food shops)

300 *ml/½ pint thick custard*
300 *ml/½ pint double cream (or a mixture of cream and Greek yoghurt), whipped*
1 *chocolate flake, crumbled*

Slice the Swiss roll and use it to line a glass trifle dish. Scatter the raspberries over the Swiss roll. Make up the jelly according to the instructions on the packet and pour it over the sponge and fruit. Chill until set. Spoon the custard evenly over the jelly, top with the cream or the cream-and-yoghurt mixture, and decorate with the crumbled flake.

Blueberry, Strawberry & Hazelnut Crumble

Everyone loves crumble and toddlers are no exception. This version is particularly irresistible and, because of the nuts, highly nutritious.

MAKES 6 ADULT PORTIONS

225 g/8 oz strawberries, washed and hulled
225 g/8 oz blueberries, washed
25 g/1 oz caster sugar
100 g/4 oz demerara sugar

100 g/4 oz toasted hazelnuts, finely chopped, or ground
100 g/4 oz wholewheat flour
100 g/4 oz butter

Place the fruit in a shallow ovenproof dish and sprinkle the caster sugar over it. Stir the demerara sugar and hazelnuts into the flour and rub in the butter. Spoon the topping over the fruit, and smooth. Bake in an oven preheated to 400°F (200°C) Gas Mark 6 for 30–40 minutes. Serve with Greek yoghurt or cream.

Bread & Butter Pudding

Another nursery classic that children love for its custard-like softness. The apricot jam makes this a little sweeter than usual; another bonus point with under-fives.

MAKES 6 ADULT PORTIONS

75 g/3 oz sultanas
30 ml/2 tablespoons orange juice
300 ml/½ pint milk
50 g/2 oz caster sugar
1 vanilla pod

3 free-range eggs
150 ml/5 fl oz double cream
8 thin slices of white bread, buttered
75 g/3 oz apricot spread

Place the sultanas and orange juice in a small bowl and leave to soak for a few hours. Heat the milk with the sugar and vanilla pod, then allow to cool before removing the vanilla pod.

Beat together the eggs and cream, then stir the cooled milk into the eggs. Spread half the bread with the jam and sandwich together with the remaining slices. Cut off the crusts. Arrange the sandwiches in a shallow ovenproof dish, sprinkling the soaked sultanas over them. Pour the milk and cream mixture over the sandwiches and leave to stand for about 1 hour. Place the dish in a deep roasting tin half-filled with hot water and bake in an oven preheated to 325°F (170°C) Gas Mark 3 for 1 hour, or until the top is crisp and golden. Serve warm rather than hot.

Spicy Apple Squares

A delicious teatime treat, these moist fruity cakes are equally good served
warm as a pudding, with custard.

MAKES 20

225 g/8 oz (prepared weight) cooking
apples, peeled, cored and chopped
100 g/4 oz caster sugar
100 g/4 oz brown sugar
75 g/3 oz mixed nuts,
finely chopped, or ground

1 teaspoon ground cinnamon
125 g/4½ oz butter
2 free-range eggs
175 g/6 oz self-raising flour
250 ml/8 fl oz sour cream

Place the apples in a pan with 25 g/1 oz of the caster sugar, cook gently until
soft, then beat to make a coarse purée. Cream together the brown sugar,
nuts, cinnamon and 40 g/1½ oz of the butter.

Cream together the remaining butter and caster sugar, beat in the eggs and
then fold in the sifted flour. Stir the sour cream into the flour mix. Grease and line
a 20 cm/8 in square cake tin, spoon in half the cake mixture and make level.
Sprinkle with half the nut mixture, then spread the apple purée on the nuts.
Cover with the remaining cake mixture and top with the remaining nut mixture.
Bake in an oven preheated to 350°F (180°C) Gas Mark 4 for 1 hour, or until firm
to touch. Cool on a wire rack.

FESTIVE FOODS

Tomato & Cheese Straws

These look pretty, taste lovely and can be dipped into anything from guacamole to yoghurt and chive dip. Be warned, however: they are rather crumbly, so take measures to protect your prized Persian carpet! Ready-rolled puff pastry is available from all major supermarkets.

MAKES 40

45 ml/3 tablespoons sun-dried tomato paste
350 g/12 oz ready-rolled puff pastry
black pepper to taste

2 teaspoons dried paprika
beaten free-range egg, to glaze
50 g/2 oz pecorino cheese, grated

Spread the sun-dried tomato paste over the pastry, season with a little pepper and sprinkle with the paprika. Fold the pastry in half, brush with beaten egg and sprinkle with pecorino. Fold in half again, then roll out to the original size. Cut into 20 long, thin strips, twist each strip several times and cut in half. Bake on a dampened baking sheet in an oven preheated to 425°F (220°C) Gas Mark 7 for 20 minutes.

☺ ☹ ❄

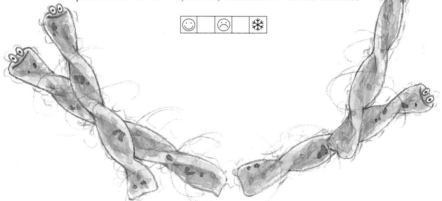

Party Pizzas

Even very young children will enjoy participating in creating their own party food. Prepare the bases and spread with tomato sauce, then let your small guests choose their own toppings. For added infant appeal, try making faces or spelling their names with pieces of vegetable and grated cheese.

MAKES 8 x 20 cm/8 in PIZZAS

DOUGH
1 kg/2 lb strong white flour
2 teaspoons salt
2 teaspoons fast-action yeast
600 ml/1 pint tepid water mixed
with 60 ml/4 tablespoons olive oil
TOMATO SAUCE
6 x 400g/14 oz cans chopped tomatoes
45 ml/3 tablespoons tomato purée

pinch of sugar
salt and black pepper to taste
TOPPINGS
mozzarella cheese, grated
fresh tomatoes, sliced
red peppers, roasted
baby sweetcorn, steamed
courgette slices, roasted
mushrooms, sautéed

Sift the flour and salt together and stir in the yeast. Make a well in the centre of the flour, pour the water and olive oil into the well and mix to form a dough. Turn on to a lightly floured board and knead for 10 minutes, or until smooth and elastic. Roll out and shape the dough into eight individual pizza bases, place on baking sheets and leave to prove in a warm place for 30 minutes.

While the dough is proving, place the tomato-sauce ingredients in a large pan, bring to the boil and simmer for 20–30 minutes until the sauce is thickened and reduced. When the sauce is cool, spread a thin layer over each pizza base. Arrange the different toppings in bowls. Allow your diminutive guests to choose their own topping preferences, then bake the pizzas in an oven preheated to 425°F (220°C) Gas Mark 7 for approximately 20 minutes.

Mini Chestnut Sausage Rolls

My son adores these with a dish of sweet mango chutney as a dip. For older children, try substituting chilli powder for the paprika.

MAKES 48 ROLLS

225 g/8 oz can unsweetened chestnut purée
1 small onion, grated
1 small apple, peeled and grated
1 clove garlic, crushed
15 ml/1 tablespoon lemon juice

15 ml/1 tablespoon soy sauce
100 g/4 oz white breadcrumbs
pinch of paprika
225 g/8 oz ready-rolled puff pastry

Combine the chestnut purée, onion, apple, garlic, lemon juice, soy sauce, breadcrumbs and paprika, and leave to stand for 30 minutes. Cut the ready-rolled pastry into strips approximately 25 mm/1 in wide. Roll the chestnut mixture into long, slim sausage shapes to fit the strips of pastry. Dampen the pastry edges, and roll the pastry strips around the chestnut sausages. Prick the pastry with a fork and cut into 25 mm/1 in lengths. Place the sausage rolls seam side down on a dampened baking sheet and bake in an oven preheated to 375°F (190°C) Gas Mark 5 for 10 minutes, or until crisp and golden.

Mini Glamorgan Sausages

Serve these tasty mini sausages cold on cocktail sticks with an Apple Purée dip,
and watch them disappear.

MAKES 16

175 g/6 oz fresh wholemeal breadcrumbs
100 g/4 oz strong Cheddar cheese, grated
1 onion, peeled and grated
1 tablespoon finely chopped flat-leaf parsley
½ teaspoon dry mustard powder

salt and black pepper to taste
1 free-range egg, beaten with a little milk
flour for coating
vegetable oil for frying

Mix together the breadcrumbs, cheese, onion, parsley, mustard and seasoning.
Bind the mixture with egg and a little milk (the amount will vary according to
how dry the breadcrumbs are). Divide the mixture into sixteen pieces, and shape
into small sausages. Roll the sausages in flour, and chill for at least 30 minutes.
Shallow- fry in a little vegetable oil until golden brown all over, about 5 minutes.

Potato Dippers

These are also known to my son as big chips, which for him makes them a
better medium for his beloved tomato sauce. Children with less predictable
palates may be persuaded to appreciate them with a sour cream and chive
dip. For children, like mine, who love garlic, crush a clove into the oil
before brushing it on the potato wedges.

MAKES 20

5 medium-sized floury potatoes
85 ml/3 fl oz olive oil
salt

Scrub the potatoes and cut each into four wedges. Boil them rapidly for 5 minutes, drain, then return them to the pan, place a lid on it and shake vigorously
(this roughens up the surfaces to ensure a crunchy result). Heat the oil in a roasting pan, add the potatoes and turn them to coat with the oil. Sprinkle with salt and
bake in an oven preheated to 425°F (220°C) Gas Mark 7 for 30–40 minutes, or until
golden and crunchy.

Mini Veggie Burgers

Parents of vegetarian children can avoid the burger issue as much as they like,
but sooner or later all toddlers will become aware of an institution called
McDonald's, and want to know why they don't eat burgers. The answer to this, of
course, is that they do – and better ones at that.

MAKES 8–10

15 ml/1 tablespoon olive oil
1 small onion, peeled and grated
1 small red pepper, seeded and finely
chopped
2 cloves garlic, finely chopped

750 g/1½ lb Vegemince, thawed
1 free-range egg, beaten
salt and black pepper to taste
flour for coating
vegetable oil for frying

Heat the oil, add the onion and pepper and fry gently until the vegetables are softened and just beginning to brown. Add the garlic, fry for a further minute and transfer the mixture to a bowl. Add the Vegemince, beaten egg and seasoning. Mix thoroughly. Shape into eight small burgers, lightly coat in flour and fry in hot oil until browned on both sides. Serve in mini bread rolls with lettuce and tomato ketchup.

Frozen Fruity Yoghurt

'I scream, you scream, everybody loves ice cream …' This scrumptious, healthy alternative freezes the spots off most commercial creations. Mango, strawberry and pineapple are good choices for the fruit purée. (Just pop the flesh in a food processor with a little sugar, if required, and whiz to a smooth pulp.)

MAKES 4–6 PORTIONS

300 ml/½ pint fruit purée
300 ml/½ pint Greek yoghurt

Whiz the fruit and yoghurt together in a food processor to combine thoroughly. Transfer to a shallow container and freeze for 1–2 hours. When ice crystals begin to form around the edge of the container, return the mixture to the food processor and blend until smooth. Return the mixture to the freezer and freeze until solid. Allow to stand at room temperature for 15 minutes before serving.

Animal Crackers

Most children find anthropomorphic eats enjoyable, so use animal-shaped
cutters to turn these biscuits into farmyard friends.

MAKES 10–16

100 g/4 oz softened butter
75 g/3 oz caster sugar
finely grated rind of ½ orange

100 g/4 oz plain flour
75 g/3 oz cornflour
40 g/1½ oz desiccated coconut

Cream together the butter, sugar and orange rind. Add the remaining ingredients
and beat to form a dough ball. Roll out the dough on a lightly floured board
and stamp out shapes using animal cutters. Place the biscuits on non-oiled baking
trays and bake in an oven preheated to 325°F (170°C) Gas Mark 3 for 15 minutes.
Cool on a wire rack.

Party People

Use currants, glacé cherries and chocolate buttons to lend character
to these face-shaped biscuits.

MAKES 40 BISCUITS

450 g/1 lb plain flour
1 teaspoon baking powder
¼ teaspoon salt
225 g/8 oz butter
200 g/7 oz caster sugar
2 free-range eggs
few drops vanilla essence

ICING
175 g/6 oz icing sugar, sifted
15 g/½ oz softened butter
20 ml/4 teaspoons boiling water
chocolate buttons, glacé cherries, currants
and vermicelli to decorate

Sift together the flour, baking powder and salt. Rub in the butter. Stir in the caster sugar. Beat the eggs with the vanilla essence and mix into the flour mixture to form a dough. Roll out the dough thinly on a lightly floured board, stamp into rounds using a 75 mm/3 in cutter and place on oiled baking sheets. Bake in an oven preheated to 350°F (180°C) Gas Mark 4 for 12 minutes until golden and beginning to brown at the edges. Cool on a wire rack. Mix together the icing ingredients and coat each biscuit smoothly. Decorate with chocolate buttons for eyes, slivers of glacé cherry for lips, currants for noses and vermicelli for hair.

Tiffin

Ridiculously rich, and irresistibly chocolatey, this tea party treat never fails to please both children and adults.

MAKES 16 PIECES

225 g/8 oz digestive biscuits
(Graham crackers), crushed
150 g/5 oz raisins
100 g/4 oz butter

25 g/1oz brown sugar
45 ml/3 tablespoons cocoa powder
60 ml/4 tablespoons golden syrup
225 g/8 oz milk or plain chocolate

Place the crushed biscuits and raisins in a large bowl. Melt the butter, sugar, cocoa powder and syrup together over a gentle heat. Combine the butter mixture with the biscuit crumbs and raisins. Press the mixture into an oiled 20 cm/8 in square tin and leave to cool. Melt the chocolate in a bowl over simmering water until smooth, then spread it over the top of the cooled biscuit mixture. Mark into squares and leave to cool thoroughly before cutting.

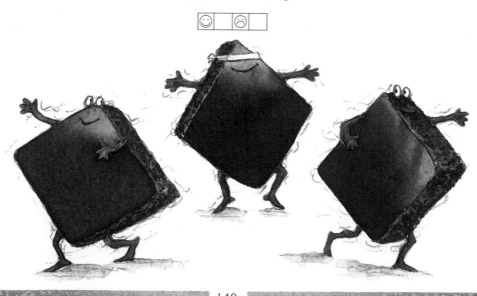

TODDLER MENU CHART

Now that your toddler is able to join in family meals, try to tailor his/her diet to fit in with yours. This suggested Menu Chart should help you plan accordingly.

INGREDIENTS CHECKLIST

Apricot spread
Baked beans
Black olives
Breads & muffins
Breakfast cereals
Brown lentils, canned
Cheese
Chocolate
Coconut milk
Condensed milk
Cream
Crisps
Digestive biscuits
Dried fruit
Eggs
Fresh fruit & vegetables
Fromage frais
Frozen vegetables
Fruit juices
Haricot beans, canned
Herbs & spices
Honey
Lasagne
Marmite/Vegemite
Mixed nuts
Molasses
Oats
Pasta shapes and rice
Peanut butter
Raspberry jelly crystals
Raspberry Swiss roll
Red kidney beans, canned
Sesame oil
Soy sauce
Sugar
Sun-dried tomato paste
Sweetcorn, canned
Tofu
Tomatoes, canned
Tomato purée
Vegetarian frankfurters, sausages & Vegemince
Yoghurt, Greek

	Breakfast	Lunch	Tea	Dinner	Bedtime
Day 1	Weetabix & banana	Stir-fried Vegetables with rice Bread & Butter Pudding	Boursin & Bean Slices Fruit	Carrot & Orange Soup Garlic Bread Yoghurt	Milk
Day 2	Scrambled egg on toast Orange segments	Vegetarian Sausage & Apple Casserole Frozen Fruity Yoghurt	Tomato & Cheese Straws Apple	Pasta with Beefless Bolognese Fruit	Milk
Day 3	Porridge with dried apricots Marmite toast	Cauliflower & Potato Bake Peas Blueberry, Strawberry & Hazelnut Crumble	Peanut Butter & Banana Fingers Fromage frais	Wild West Beans Vegetarian hot dogs Fruit	Milk
Day 4	Muffin Rabbits Peach or pear	Vegetable Curry with banana, yoghurt & rice Fruit	Italian Flag Rolls Spicy Apple Squares	Potato Dippers Salad Fromage frais	Milk
Day 5	Toasted Haloumi cheese & tomato sandwich Fruit	Spinach & Mushroom Lasagne Salad Yoghurt	Potato Cakes Apple Purée Raspberry Trifle	Frittata Baked beans Fruit	Milk
Day 6	Cornflakes Strawberries Cinnamon toast	Paella Thomas' Lemon Flan	Mini Veggie Burgers Fruit	Leek Tart Tomato salad Fromage frais	Milk
Day 7	Boiled egg with Marmite soldiers Grapes	Bread & Cheese Pudding Grated apple & carrot salad Yoghurt	Baked Potato with Ratatouille Chocolate Baked Bananas	Four Seasons Soup Cheese & Herb Scones Fruit	Milk

INDEX

THE VEGETARIAN SOCIETY

The Vegetarian Society exists to promote and provide information on a vegetarian diet for the benefit of animal welfare, human health and the environment. Established in 1847, the Society is the acknowledged expert on vegetarianism and all aspects relating to the diet, and produces information sheets, leaflets, videos and other material.

Members of the Society receive a full-colour high-quality magazine each quarter and a card offering discounts at establishments ranging from health-food stores, restaurants and guesthouses, to fancy-dress hire and roadside rescue. The Society provides a range of diverse services, as well as its unique seedling logo badge, reduced-rate subscription to BBC *Vegetarian Good Food* or *Wildlife* magazines and exclusive access to the Society's free information hotline. It offers all members the opportunity to get actively involved if desired, either through the Society's network of 150 local groups or through the Council of Trustees, elected from the members.

The Society also runs its own cookery school, Cordon Vert, which provides day, weekend and week courses ranging from our Diploma course and professional tuition to leisure courses for the beginner or the adventurous cook wanting to expand their repertoire.

The Society works with major food manufacturers and retailers to improve the quality, quantity and variety of vegetarian food available and administers its own license scheme for approved products.

To receive further information write to The Vegetarian Society, Parkdale, Dunham road, Altrincham, Cheshire, WA14 4QG. Or telephone and join by credit card on 0161 928 0793. The Society's e-mail address is vegsoc@vegsoc.demon.co.uk and its web site can be visited at http://www.vegsocuk.org.

• •

EDDISON • SADD EDITIONS

Editor................Vivienne Wells
Proof reader.........Nikky Twyman
Indexer..............Dorothy Frame
Art Director.....Elaine Partington
Art Editor.............Pritty Ramjee
Illustrator............Stephen May
Production..........Hazel Kirkman and Katrina Macnab